Financial Planning for Retirement and Beyond

How to Finance the Rest of Your Life

Edward M. Wolpert

Published by Oconee Financial Planning Services LLC www.oconeefps.com

This book is intended to provide authoritative and useful information. It represents the opinions and ideas of the author and is in no way a recommendation to purchase or sell stock and/or options in general, or of any particular company. Further, nothing contained herein is meant to be construed as financial or tax advice. The author and publisher hereby specifically disclaim any responsibility for any possible liability, loss, risk, personal or otherwise, which might be incurred as a consequence, whether directly or indirectly, of the use and/or application of any of the content of this book.

Cover design by Cheryl Klinginsmith

ISBN 978-0-9800769-4-3

Printed in the United States of America

Table of Contents

Preface

This book has as its intended audience adults in their 40s though 70s. I had not originally planned to write this book. I had written *The Young Adult's Guide to Financial Success* in 2009 as a response to the dearth of financial information available to young adults in their teens, 20s, and 30s. The wide acceptance of that book by its intended audience was gratifying. Then, a local church asked me to make a presentation for members in this age group. I was happy to do so. But they also wanted a presentation for older folks who were staring retirement in the face. Could I do something for them?

I told them I would work something up. I suggested the title, "Financial Success for Seniors" but they nixed that. Apparently they thought that the 40s, 50s, 60s, and 70s group might not be thrilled at being referred to as "seniors." So they suggested the title, "Financial Planning for Retirement and Beyond." I developed the presentation with that title, and after the session, I was encouraged to write a book for this age group in the same style and manner of the *Young Adult's* book.

So, this is it.

The problem I faced is that, unlike the target audience of *The Young Adult's Guide*—late teens, 20s, and 30s something—this book was aimed at a wider audience later in their lives. Of course, as one ages, life gets more complex, financially as well as in other ways. I wanted to be sure that essential information would be provided for all target readers. So, I've included some basic information as well as a discussion of complex issues, which goes well beyond the basics.

Chapter One introduces the idea of financial planning, and the factors you must consider. Chapter Two deals with the development of a balance sheet and a cash flow statement. No matter what your age or wealth status, in order to plan you have to know what you already have, and what's coming in. Chapters Three and Four deal with basic information about investing, and the financial instruments used in this endeavor. Chapter Five discusses portfolio investing. Most people will use mutual funds to invest in an existing portfolio, but there are alternative funds as well.

Chapters Six and Seven discuss the benefits of tax deferring, and in particular, deal with several retirement structures that take advantage of such deferring. Chapter Eight discusses the need for, and the means with which to protect your assets.

Chapter Nine and Ten get right into the nitty-gritty of financing your retirement and beyond. Discussed will be the decisions you must make, and the specifics as to how to make your plan. Also included are ideas for dealing with money not needed for your retirement.

Chapter Eleven is a frank presentation of the subject of taxation. The subtitle to the chapter is "The Wild Card." And indeed it is. The book closes with Chapter Twelve that deals with how to select a financial advisor if needed. Three appendices are offered to provide additional resources if needed.

With this book, my goal is to provide to readers a comprehensive presentation of what's involved in financial planning for retirement, so they will be well informed about the financial issues relevant to this portion of their lives. Retirement should be your golden years, but you need to have some gold to enjoy it.

This book was written in the second half of 2013. Since the turn of this century, we have witnessed some extraordinary economic volatility. Indeed, the 2008 financial meltdown almost turned into an economic rout comparable to the Great Depression. The Fed Funds rate is close to zero as I write, and bonds, which in more normal times could be used to gain income with some stability in the value of the principal, are questionable investments. Hopefully, in the next five to eight years, interest rates will revert to their more normal, historic returns.

Also note that in the examples presented, and in the projections made in this book, I use a return of 6%. With my emphasis on common stocks as the long-term investment medium of choice, I believe that over time, a return of 6% is reasonable; indeed, it is probably on the low side. As a rule, and especially so in planning, I'd rather be conservative in my estimates than make pie-in-the-sky projections.

My thanks go to Steve Erikson, Yisrel Cotlar, and J. J. Arias for their unique contributions to the book. Beth Roberts did a superb job of editing. All errors of omission and commission are mine.

Edward M. Wolpert
November 2013
Decatur, Georgia

Chapter One

Introduction

Congratulations. If you are reading this book, you are taking seriously your financial future, especially your retirement. As with any endeavor, planning for retirement requires projections and predictions about the future, which may or may not be what actually occurs. But, plan we must, because to do otherwise invites calamities that might have been avoided.

The Phases of Your Financial Life

There are four distinct but overlapping phases of your financial life:

1. Growing up and getting educated. For most people, there is not too much happening financially in this phase, since someone else is usually supporting them. Thus, this phase is mostly preparatory for earning a living. However, college students often incur substantial debt during the college years that can impact their finances for years, if not decades.

2. Accumulation. It is during this period that people start earning their livings and acquiring asset bases for retirement and beyond.

3. Accumulation and maintenance. Here people continue to accumulate assets, but also seek to maintain their wealth by allocating their assets perhaps differently than before.

4. Retirement. At this point, people look at where they are in their lives, and make decisions about their financial needs for their remaining years.

The approach to financial planning for retirement is deliberate, informed, focused, linear, and sequential. You can't go into retirement without having planned for this time, and those who don't plan may be very disappointed. Their "golden years" may not to be so golden. While you can't predict the future with any certainty, unless you're very, very, lucky, with no plan at all, retirement can be a financial disaster.

Pre-Planning

Before actually doing the financial planning, there are several important questions that must be answered. They have to do with your goals and desires, and your present and anticipated financial status. And typically, each question includes many sub-questions that must be addressed.

Some questions are philosophical, some are technical, and some are future projections, but each question is important, and all of them are related to one another. They must be considered collectively as well as individually.

What are your financial goals?
Do you want to have enough money to live well now, and have less money for a financially secure retirement? Or are you more concerned with retirement? Are there things you want to do before retirement that will take substantial financial resources? Are you willing to forego the future for the present, or forego the present for the future? Or balance the two?

What is the current status of your wealth?
This, of course, is the starting point for any projections of future wealth. Regardless of where it came from, how much wealth do you already have? Are you expecting significant inheritances or other windfalls?

What is your anticipated cash flow?
This is related to your wealth status. How much money is presently coming into your household, and how much is being spent? Are you living within your means? Do you, or will you, have extra cash with which to build your wealth? Do you expect to be earning significantly more money in the future?

What is your anticipated longevity?
In other words, how long do you expect to live? What is the current status of your health? If you have health issues, are they of a type that will impact your longevity? What is your current lifestyle in terms of exercise, diet, and stress? Assuming death from natural causes, how old were your parents and grandparents when they died? How long do you think you want to live?

When do you plan to retire?
The first sub-question is, "Do you want to retire?" And related to that is, "Will you be able to afford to completely retire?" Some people continue working because they enjoy their work, or because they need the extra income, or both. At some point, you'll need to set a time, a target date to aim at, to allow for

meaningful planning to occur. For many people, age 65 is the starting point for these deliberations, probably because that's when full benefit Social Security used to kick in.[1] Now, the full benefits are delayed to age 66 or later, although earlier receipt of benefits, albeit at a lower amount, is still available at age 62.

What kind of life style do you expect to have in retirement?
Do you want to maintain the standard of living you've had during your working years? Or raise it? Or settle for a lifestyle requiring less money? Do you expect to live in the same city, or perhaps in the same house?

How much income do you think you'll need?
Look at how much it costs for your present, pre-retirement life style. Will you need more than that? Less than that? About the same?

Do you expect to have any dependents at the time of retirement?
Your pre-retirement years may have included dependent children or other family members. Will these persons be dependent on you at retirement? Is it possible, or perhaps probable, that in retirement years you would be called upon to finance the raising of your grandchildren? Or to care for your parents?

What are your anticipated sources of retirement income?
In past generations, when people planned for retirement, they saw the funding as a three legged stool: Leg #1, Social Security. Leg #2, an employer pension. Leg #3, personal savings. Now, however, Social Security remains as a leg, but it may be received later than expected, and taxed more heavily. Employer pensions, the "old-fashioned" defined-benefit pension based upon years of service and highest salary, are disappearing from the private sector. They are mostly being replaced by defined contribution plans (e.g. 401(k) plans) that are funded by pre-tax contributions from the employer and the employee. Personal savings remain an important leg of the stool.

---

1   Otto von Bismarck, the first Chancellor of the German Empire, introduced old age and disability pensions in 1889. This was the first such program in the world. The retirement age was originally 70, but in 1917 it was reduced to 65. The average life span at the end of the 19th century was about 50.

These are questions only you can answer. The next two questions will be answered in part by the contents of this book.

How should you deploy your assets to achieve your income requirements?
That depends upon your risk tolerance and time horizon. What is your risk tolerance? And your time horizon? Generally speaking, the longer the time until the funds are needed, the more risk you can take on. That's because if a risky investment goes sour, there's still time to make it right. On the other hand, the closer you come to needing the funds, the less risky your investments should be.

What will you do with unneeded assets in retirement while alive?
Do you want to leave a large estate to your heirs? Do you want to spend it? Give it away? The problem of what to do with your unneeded wealth is a wonderful problem to have, but needs to be addressed at some time.

With careful consideration of these questions, and resolution of the issues they represent, you are ready to begin the financial planning process. Let's see where you are with regard to your personal financial situation.

Chapter Two

Your Present Financial Status

Now that you've asked (and hopefully answered) some basic questions, the next order of business is to determine the status of your wealth, and then your cash flow.

The prime document in determining your wealth is a balance sheet. It shows, at a given time, your assets (what you own), your liabilities (what you owe), and the difference between them, referred to as net worth. The formula is easy and straightforward:

$$\text{Assets} - \text{Liabilities} = \text{Net Worth}$$

Or, with a touch of algebra, we can restate it as

$$\text{Assets} = \text{Liabilities} + \text{Net Worth}$$

Development of a Balance Sheet

When developing a balance sheet, you should classify your assets and liabilities with regard to their function and type. And when you look at your completed balance sheet, it can tell you one of two possible things about your overall financial position. Your net worth can be:

- Positive, meaning you have more assets than liabilities.
- Negative, meaning your liabilities exceed your assets. In other words, you're in debt.

Valuing Your Assets

In the examples show below in Figures 2-1 and 2-2, notice that there are two categories of assets: financial assets, and use assets. That's the first categorization. Then, it's a good idea to sub-categorize your financial assets into non-retirement financial assets, and retirement financial assets.

The values for the financial assets can be taken from the latest statements of the institutions that hold them. The values for the use assets should be your estimate of their market value, that is, what a perfect stranger might pay for them. The value of your liabilities can be taken from the most recent statements from your creditors.

Figure 2-1
Harry and Monica Clement - Balance Sheet, April 4, 2014
(All assets and liabilities are held jointly unless otherwise specified)

ASSETS		
Financial Assets (Non-Retirement)		
Checking Account	$2,752	
Savings Account	15,879	
Treasury Bonds	20,000	
CDs	10,000	
Large Cap Mutual Fund	97,451	
Small Cap Mutual Fund	33,618	
Total Non-Retirement Financial Assets		**$179,700**
Financial Assets (Retirement)		
403(b) (Harry)	$38,902	
401(k) (Monica)	42,029	
IRA (Harry)	31,922	
IRA (Monica)	33,356	
Rollover IRA (Harry)	16,936	
Total Retirement Financial Assets		**$163,145**
Total Financial Assets		**$342,845**
Use Assets		
Residence	$420,000	
Furniture/Household Goods	10,000	
Vehicle #1	8.500	
Vehicle #2	17,000	
Total Use Assets		**$455,500**
TOTAL ASSETS		**$798,345**
LIABILITIES		
Mortgage Loan	$205,912	
Vehicle #2 Loan	5,895	
Credit Card Debt (Avg. Monthly Balance)	750	
Total Liabilities		**$212,557**
NET WORTH		**$585,788**
TOTAL LIABILITIES AND NET WORTH		**$798,345**

Harry and Monica Clement

Figure 2-1 is an example of a balance sheet for a fictional couple, Harry and Monica Clement. They are in their mid-forties and expect to retire when they are age 65.

Let's take a look at the Clements' balance sheet. Overall, they are in pretty good shape with a net worth of $585,788. Their non-retirement assets total $179,700, which means that there would be ready cash in case one of them loses a job, or some other calamity occurs. They are both taking advantage of the current tax law by having $163,145 in tax-deferred accounts. Their liabilities are few and are reasonable as they seek to pay off big purchases, their house and a vehicle. To have a net worth of more than a half million dollars in your mid-forties is to be well positioned for a financially secure retirement.

What will they be worth in 20 years at age 65? Presently, the total of their financial assets is $342,845. At an annual growth rate of 6%, and assuming $5,000 annual increases to their financial assets, in 20 years, the value of their financial assets will be $1,294,514. Not bad! If they did not make the annual contribution of $5,000, the value would be $1,099,550. Still pretty good. In Chapter Nine, we'll see how that plays out.

Mark and Cindy Travers

Figure 2-2 is the balance sheet of Mark and Cindy Travers, a couple in their early 30s.

The Travers couple has assets totaling $491,494. They seem to be living the good life. They live in a house they own, drive fairly new cars, have an RV, and a boat. They have accumulated an assortment of physical things. Unfortunately however, they have also accumulated a lot of debt. They have a negative net worth: they owe more than they own.

Not only is their house mortgaged to the hilt, $350,00 of debt (first and second mortgages) on a house valued at $370,000, but also they have large amounts of credit card debt, as well as car, RV, and boat loans. As a result of this debt, they have a net worth of negative $1,553. Also, they don't have very much cash or cash equivalents on hand in case of an emergency, only $4,6,16. They are not in good financial shape, but they are young enough to reform their spending habits and prepare for a decent retirement.

7

Figure 2-2
Mark and Cindy Travers - Balance Sheet, November 4, 2014
(All assets and liabilities are held jointly unless otherwise specified)

ASSETS		
Financial Assets (Non-Retirement)		
Checking Account	$1,278	
Savings Account	3,338	
Total Non-Retirement Financial Assets		**$4,616**
Financial Assets (Retirement)		
401(k) (Mark)	$12,927	
401(k) (Cindy)	16,451	
Total Retirement Financial Assets		**$29,378**
Total Financial Assets		**$33,994**
Use Assets		
Residence	$370,000	
RV	13,000	
Boat	20,500	
Furniture/Household Goods	7,500	
Vehicle #1 (Cindy)	22.500	
Vehicle #2 (Mark)	19,500	
Jewelry	4,500	
Total Use Assets		**$457,500**
TOTAL ASSETS		**$491,494**
LIABILITIES		
Mortgage Loan	$329,420	
Second Mortgage Loan	20,580	
RV Loan	13,750	
Boat Loan	15,000	
Credit Card (Cindy)	47,720	
Credit Card (Mark)	32,561	
Car Loan #1	18,588	
Car Loan #2	15,428	
Total Liabilities		**$493,047**
NET WORTH		**($1,553)**
TOTAL LIABILITIES AND NET WORTH		**$491,494**

With the help of a financial advisor, they made a plan to change their spending and borrowing habits. They sold off their RV and boat, and paid off the loans on them. They paid off the second mortgage loan on their residence, and renegotiated the terms of their first mortgage. They paid off their credit cards and decided to live within their income and build wealth with the excess. They started IRAs. And by age 40, they had net financial assets of $85,000.

What will they be worth in 32 years at age 65? Presently, the total of their financial assets is $85,000. At an annual growth rate of 6%, and assuming $5,000 annual increases to their financial assets, in 32 years, the value of their financial assets will be $1,038,254. If they did not make the annual contribution of $5,000, the value would be $548,538. In Chapter Nine, we'll see how that plays out.

Cash Flow Analysis
Before developing our understanding of cash flow, we need to consider the difference between wealth and income.

Wealth and Income
Wealth and income are two related terms used to describe a person's financial status. We might say that a person is wealthy, or that a person has a high income. Both statuses are desirable, but they are different. You can be 1) wealthy with high income, 2) wealthy with low income, 3) not wealthy with high income, and 4) and not wealthy with low income. Of course, in terms of financial status, most people would like to be wealthy and have a high income.

Are "riches" the same as wealth? Yes. Remember the character Tevya in the 1963 Broadway musical Fiddler on the Roof? One of his songs begins, "If I were a rich man..." The song ends with "...if I were a wealthy man." So, in common parlance, to be wealthy is to be rich. Wealth and riches, the terms are used interchangeably.

But wealth and income are two different things. Wealth is what you already have. Income is what's coming in. That seems simple enough. So, why the confusion between these two words? The two concepts are used interchangeably and erroneously by some folks. Some of our political leaders (in both parties) say that they want to "tax the rich." And when asked about how to define the rich, they'll say that rich people have a household income of $400,000 for a single taxpayer, and $450,000 for a couple. However, people who earn those salaries are not necessarily rich. Yes, they have above average compensation. You could call them well compensated. But rich? Perhaps, but perhaps not.

I know people, perhaps you do, too, who are well compensated, spend all their income, and have no savings or investments to show for it. They are not rich. They have income but not wealth. On the other hand, I know people who have modest income, but have amassed significant wealth. They are rich. But these are not the people our elected officials have identified to pay higher taxes.[1]

Income Begets Wealth, and Wealth Begets Income

So, how do you get a good income? For most people, it means having a job that will pay you well. And how do you get wealth? Excluding the possibility of windfalls such as a large inheritance or winning the lottery, you can simply spend less than you earn, and save the rest. At first, a savings account might be best. Then invest in any of variety of financial instruments. Most financial instruments will kick off dividends, interest, or capital gains. This is income. It can be spent as other income that you earned through your vocation, or it can be reinvested to increase the value of your wealth. Thus, your wealth is derived originally from your income, and subsequently it adds to your income.

Your balance sheet shows the extent and configuration of your wealth. Now we turn our attention to your cash flow statement that deals with your income.

Developing Your Cash Flow Statement

A cash flow statement is composed of two parts: cash-in, and cash-out. Cash-in is your salary, tips, royalties, dividends, gambling winnings, etc., in short, anything that you would list as income on your Federal 1040 tax return. Each source of funds is identified and a dollar amount is assigned. Cash-out shows what you do with your income. Each expenditure is identified and assigned a dollar amount. Any difference between cash-in and cash-out is considered discretionary income. This is the money that will develop or add to your wealth.

---

1   Not yet, anyway. More on that in Chapter Eleven.

In a typical household unit, there are a few sources of income such as salaries, fees, commissions, dividends, interest, etc. So the cash-in section of the statement will be fairly short. In contrast however, the cash-out section will often have twenty or more entries.

For our first couple, Harry and Monica Clement, it's probably not necessary for them to itemize every expenditure. They live within their means, and from the look of their balance sheet, they have been acquiring significant assets, without incurring very much debt. They have some wealth, $585,788. They can track their expenses to see if they were wasting any money, which, if not wasted, would add to their wealth.

On the other hand, we have Mark and Cindy Travers whose balance sheet shows a negative net worth of $1,553. They cannot go on spending the way they have been spending, because sooner or later they will have such a debt burden that they will need to declare bankruptcy. Clearly, they must do something about their spending, so a detailed cash flow statement would be in order.[2] They will need to have an accurate picture as to how much money they have coming in, and where that money is going. Based on this information, they can set up a budget, and resolve to stick to it.

They will probably have to sell off some assets (e.g. the boat and the RV), use the proceeds to pay down their debt, and organize their lives in such a way as to allow the development of discretionary income to further pay down debt, and then make a plan for the accumulation of wealth. Fortunately, they are in their late thirties and have time to make things right before retirement.

Next Steps

After you have developed your balance sheet and cash flow analyses, you need to decide approximately when you will retire, and make a conservative projection of what your financial situation will be at that time. Then, list the potential sources of retirement income. This might include the following:

- Social Security
- Employer retirement plan(s)

---

2   For a detailed explanation of how to develop a cash flow statement and a budget, see Appendix A

- Individual Retirement Account(s)
- Savings and investments
- Other sources

At this point, you may be able to determine whether, at retirement time, there will be enough money to live in the style that you want. Of course, the further away from the retirement date you are, the less accurate your projections might be. But it's a good idea to start thinking about this now.

Chapter Three

Saving and Investing

In the previous two chapters, we were introduced to the questions we need to ask ourselves, and how to describe our financial status. This chapter picks up from there as we present information about how wealth is created and deployed to meet our goals.

After retirement funding through employment-related accounts, Social Security, and individual retirement funds, the final category is non-retirement funds. Most of this money will be the result of prudent investing during your pre-retirement years. This investing is done to create wealth to be used for retirement funding, or for any other purpose you choose.

The term "wealth" as used here refers to financial wealth, also known as money or riches. As described in Chapter Two, the beginning of wealth occurs when your income exceeds your expenses. The difference between the two is the start of wealth. What can you do with wealth? You can keep it, spend it, or give it away. Of course, before you retire, your focus should be on keeping it. If you keep it, where should you put it so it will grow? How should it be invested?

Fundamental Concepts of Investing
In order to choose the appropriate action to deploy wealth to increase it, there are some fundamental concepts of which you need to be aware. Understanding these concepts makes your decision process regarding investing informed, and more likely to succeed.

Risk and Reward
Risk is the chance you take that you will lose some or all of your investment. *Reward* is the benefit you get from saving or investing, and usually comes in the form of money received as dividends, interest, or in the profits (realized or unrealized) from the increase in an asset's value. Bank accounts bear virtually no risk, indeed they may be insured, but they don't offer much reward, either.

The most fundamental concept in investing is that as risk increases, so does potential reward. And, conversely, as reward increases, so does potential risk. This is an immutable law. There are no exceptions. You don't get something for nothing in financial matters, and if someone promises you a "guaranteed" high financial reward for little or no risk, run, don't walk, away. It just ain't gonna happen.

Liquidity

This refers to the ease with which you can convert your investment into cash, either greenbacks or a checking account. Vehicles like checking accounts are very *liquid*, indeed, they may define liquidity. On the other hand, real estate, collectables, or thinly traded bonds are considered illiquid. They cannot be readily converted to cash.

The most liquid vehicles where money can be placed are checking accounts, savings accounts, money market accounts, and short term CDs. These have virtually no risk (but also comparatively low rewards), and are appropriate for persons who
* are extremely averse to risk (very low risk tolerance), or
* have a short time horizon, or
* need instant liquidity.

Money that might be needed for an emergency should be placed in savings vehicles such as those described above. Emergencies do happen: you lose your job, your car breaks down, your water heater goes kaput, etc. Money for this purpose should be in a savings or money market account, since you have a short time horizon and liquidity is essential.

On the other hand, suppose you already have money put away, liquid assets, for an emergency such as a lost job. However, you plan to buy a car in about a year. Money for that purpose can be put in a CD that has a twelve-month maturity. This financial instrument will give you a better return than the checking or savings account.

Compound Interest

Albert Einstein is reported to have said, "The most powerful force in the universe is compound interest." It certainly is powerful. It gets its power from adding interest to the principal, and then computing interest on the new, larger principal, and continuing to do so.

Which would you rather have: $1,000,000 now or two cents which would double every day for 30 days? Trick question, right? Personally, I'd rather have the two cents with daily doubling. Doubling means 100% interest compounding daily for 30 days. After thirty days, your two cents would have compounded to $1,073,741,824. Not bad for two cents!

The Magic of Compounding

The example above shows the magic of compounding. But compounding needs time to do its work, as just seen. After one day, you'd have four cents. After two days, you'd have eight cents. In wealth enhancement, time is your ally, so the sooner you can begin, the better.

To demonstrate this principle, let's look at some examples that have meaning in financial planning. All examples assume payments made at the beginning of each month, monthly compounding, and a 6% annual interest rate.

Table 3-1
Results of $100 Monthly Investments, Compounded at 6%

Years of Compounding	Total Amount Invested	Value at End of Period
20	$24,000	$46,204
30	$36,000	$100,450
40	$48,000	$199,149

Take a look at Table 3-1. This shows the results of making monthly investments of $100 with compounding at the rate of 6%. The first column shows the number of years in which these monthly investments compounded. The second column shows the total amount invested in that period. The third column shows the value of that amount at the end of the period.

As you can see from the table, in 20 years you would have contributed $24,000, which would have grown to $46,204 at the end of the 20 years. Similar data are shown for 30 and 40 years. But note carefully the ratios of years of compounding to the values at the end of the period. The ten-year increase of amounts invested from 20 years to 30 years, $24,000 to $36,000, is an increase of 50%. But the value of the investment at the ends of these periods, the increase from $46,204 to $100,450, represents an increase of 117%. Even more dramatic is the increase from 20 years to 40 years of compounding. The increase of amounts invested from 20 years to 40 years, $24,000 to $48,000, is an increase of 100%. But the value of the investment at the ends of these periods, from $46,204 to $199,149, represents an increase of 331%%.

Tables 3-2 and 3-3 show similar data for monthly contributions of $300 and $500 respectively. The ratios of years of compounding to values at the end of the period are the same. The values, of course, are larger, because the amounts invested are larger.

Table 3-2
Results of $300 Monthly Contributions, Compounded at 6%

Years of Compounding	Total Amount Invested	Value at End of Period
20	$72,000	$138,612
30	$108,000	$301,355
40	$144,000	$597,447

Table 3-3
Results of $500 Monthly Contributions, Compounding at 6%

Years of Compounding	Total Amount Invested	Value at End of Period
20	$120,000	$231,020
30	$186,000	$502,258
40	$240,000	$995,745

Now, take a look at Table 3-4. This table extracts data from Tables 3-1 and 3-2 and shows how time is your ally.

Table 3-4
Comparison of Two Investment Strategies

Monthly Investment	Years of Compounding	Total Amount Invested	Value at End of period
$100	40	$24,000	$199,149
$300	20	$72,000	$138,612

Table 3-4 shows that $100 per month compounding for 40 years, results in more value, $199,149, than $300 per month compounding for 20 years, $138,612. Thus, you can often do better putting in less money earlier, than more money later. In other words, a part of your financial success is not just a question of how <u>much</u> you invest, it's how <u>early</u> you start investing.

For example, remember the two couples in Chapter Two, Harry and Monica Clement, and Mark and Cindy Travers? The Clements had $342,845 invested 20 years before retirement. At a compounding rate of 6%, and with no additional contributions, that figure increased by $786,705, to $1,099,550, an increase of 221% in 20 years. Mark and Cindy Travers had $85,000 invested for 32 years before retirement. That figure increased by $463,538 to $548, 538, an increase of 545%. These data are summarized in Table 3-5.

Table 3-5
Comparison of Two Couples' Retirement Values, Compounding at 6%

Investing Couple	Initial Investment	Years Compounding	Earnings	Value at Retirement	Increase
Clements	$342,845	20	$786,705	$1,099,550	221%
Traverses	$85,000	32	$463,538	$548,538	545%

A Word of Caution

It should be noted that the examples shown in the tables above represent hypothetical scenarios. Variations in earnings rates, taxes, and inflation have not been factored in. In reality, the values at the end of the period would vary somewhat from the figures presented, and of course, the purchasing power of those figures would be diminished by even a slow rate of inflation. Notwithstanding these factors, continuous compounding is a strong and useful tool in accumulating wealth.

Savings vs. Investing

Saving, that is, accumulating money, is a good place to start financial independence. Money saved can be stored in a coffee can buried in your backyard, or perhaps under a mattress. Assuming no one finds out about this cache of cash, your money will be safe. However, if history is any guide, as time goes on, the money will have less purchasing power due to the deleterious effects of inflation. So the coffee can idea has limited merit. Besides, it's inconvenient to go digging in the dirt behind your house.

Banks[1] can be helpful here. They will accept deposits of your money and put it in an account that you can access as needed. If it's a checking account, you'll have immediate access to it, and they may pay you a little interest. If it's a savings account, there may be some restrictions on the money's accessibility, but you'll be paid more interest than a checking account. Another possible account is a money market account, on which interest is paid, but generally there is a limit on the number or minimum amounts of checks written on the account. You may also purchase a Certificate of Deposit (CD) at a bank. There may be further restrictions regarding accessibility, but you'll be paid more interest than the other accounts just mentioned. Most banks are members of the Federal Deposit Insurance Corporation (FDIC), and your money will be insured up to a maximum of $250,000. If the bank fails, the FDIC will make you whole.[2]

Bank accounts and CDs represent a source of ready cash. This is for paying your bills, but also in anticipation of a possible loss of employment.

These bank accounts are some ways to begin saving money. If the accounts are insured, there is no risk involved. However, interest rates will differ among the various accounts for savings. Your checking account will probably pay you the lowest interest rate, so keep enough money in it to pay for your regular monthly expenses with a small margin for safety. Next is your savings account, which pays more interest than your checking account. Keep money in this account for emergencies, or for anticipated expenditures that will occur within the year. For expected expenditures in time periods longer than one year, save money in one or more certificates of deposit (CDs). They pay the highest interest.

If you are fortunate, the interest you will receive in the savings and CD accounts will exceed the rate of inflation, so you will have little or no risk of losing purchasing power to inflation, although this is rarely the case.

Investing

When you have accumulated some wealth through savings, and have made provision for emergencies, you should begin to invest the remainder of your wealth.

---

1   The term banks, as used here, includes credit unions, and savings and loans institutions
2   The National Credit Union Administration (NCUA), a government agency, insures accounts in credit unions. Coverage is similar to that provided by the FDIC.

A good place to start is investing in financial instruments: stocks and bonds. Both of these asset categories have their place in your personal investments, and will be explained in detail in Chapter Four.

The first consideration before any action is taken, is when you'll need the money invested, that is, your time horizon. The second consideration is how to allocate your wealth into asset classes.

The Importance of Time Horizon in Investment Decisions

You are investing money with the idea that when you will need it, it will be there for you and be valued at more than you paid for it. You might need it soon, or perhaps later.

In a random assortment of several dozen retirees or pre-retirees, it would be rare to find any two households who would need the same advice. There would be substantial differences among them regarding their wealth, income, risk tolerance, time horizon, and a myriad of other personal and financial issues. Thus, no one mix of assets is appropriate for everyone. In today's financial markets and in general, I believe that stocks will do better in the long run than bonds in creating wealth as they have historically, and that bonds should be used to provide current income when needed and/or to add ballast to your portfolio.

As an example, consider these two fictional cases.

Case #1. Sam and Dorothy Whitlock. Sam and Dorothy are both retired professionals. They have three grown children and two grandchildren. They have net assets in excess of $2.5 million. They own their house and they have no debt. Each has a defined benefit pension which when combined with their Social Security benefits gives them cash flow of $2,500 per month without tapping their non-retirement financial assets and this cash income covers their needs and wants with a little left over. They are in good health and are expecting to live another 25 years. They have moderate risk tolerance.

Based on this information, Sam and Dorothy probably should be mostly invested in stocks. They have no need for the income produced by bonds.

Case #2. Harry and Ethel Slocum. Harry and Ethel recently retired, he from a sales position with a computer manufacturer, and she from a marketing position with the same company. They have two grown children and two grandchildren one of whom has serious health problems. They have 401(k) plans and IRAs from which they intend to draw benefits, as well as their Social Security. Their cash flow from their retirement assets and Social Security is $700 per month short of covering their needs and wants. Aside from their 401(k)s and IRAs they have net assets of $250,000. They own their house and have little debt. They are in good health and expect to live another 20 years. They have moderate risk tolerance.

Asset Allocation

For the readers of this book, the two classes of assets we will be considering are stocks and bonds. Asset allocation refers to the proportion of each asset class in the totality of your financial instruments.

It would be worthwhile to remove from your thinking such rules of thumb such as "Your percentage mix of stocks and bonds should be 80/20 when you are young, and 20/80 when you are retired." This is too facile and not necessarily appropriate for a given individual. There are also formulas like, "Subtract your age from 100 and that should be the percentage of stocks you should have in your portfolio." Again, I believe such thinking is the wrong way to go. No formula will work for everyone.

When you have a full understanding of your financial situation and your anticipated needs for cash, the question is how will you allocate your assets to meet your anticipated needs. In your thinking, you can divide your cash needs into short-term or long-term.

For case #1, Sam and Dorothy Whitlock, their needs are covered with their anticipated cash flow and have no need for income producing assets. They can think long-term.

For case #2, Harry and Ethel Slocum, they will need $700 per month additional cash flow to meet their financial needs. They will need to think both short-term and long-term.

You can see by these two examples how asset allocation needs to be customized for the idiosyncratic differences in the two situations. Other issues to be considered are whether the couples want to give financial assistance to their children and/or grandchildren; whether helping with college and/or medical expenses for them is something they want to do. The list could go on and on, but I'm sure you get the picture.

Short-Term Investing

Suppose, within the next three to five years, you anticipate needing a certain amount of money for a down payment on a house, or for tuition expenses, or for some elective surgery, etc. You have the money now, but you want to be sure you are able to access it—all of it—when you want it, and at its present or increased value.

Fixed income instruments are the ticket: savings accounts, money market accounts, or CDs, would be the best. You might get some interest on them. So, the money will be there. Bonds, however, are not recommended, because they can vary in value. The same goes for equities. When you need the money, the value of bonds or equities may be less than what they were when you first invested in them. Thus, converting them into cash might incur a loss.

However, if you buy bonds, which mature on dates when you will need the cash, and plan on holding them to maturity, such bonds may be appropriate. You can build a ladder from them with staggered maturities as needed. Or, you could do the same thing with CDs.

Long Term Investing

Investing for the long-term, more than five years, is more nuanced than short-term investing. During the period after five years, will you need income? If so, how much? If you won't need income, will you take moderate risk to increase the value of your assets? Depending upon the amount of cash needed, you could build a ladder of bonds (held to maturity as described above) and/or CDs. Or you could invest in equities that have a steady and predictable dividend yield, so you could benefit from capital gains in the equities as well as receiving the needed income.

Chapter Four

Understanding Financial Investments

This chapter will give a brief overview of financial investments that are available to and appropriate for you, the retail investor. If you have been investing for some time, you might want to skip this chapter.

Basically, there are two types of financial instruments: fixed income and equities.[1]

Fixed-Income

This is a broad category that includes a variety of financial instruments. What they all have in common is that they represent an indebtedness of the issuing entity. Also, the income from them is usually fixed, that is, it doesn't (or shouldn't) vary with the revenues of the entity. Moreover, the intrinsic value of these instruments can be easily computed with the knowledge of a few significant data. Fixed income securities are generally considered to be a more conservative type of financial investment than are equities.

Bonds

The most significant of the fixed-income financial instruments is bonds. Bonds are financial instruments that represent the indebtedness of the issuing entity to the bondholder. Various entities issue bonds:
• Federal government,
• Cities, towns, municipalities, and states,
• Corporations.

Bonds are issued at a par value (the amount borrowed and to be repaid), and with a stated interest payment (the coupon), and with a maturity date (the date on which the bond must be repaid). They are rated by one of three rating agencies as to the probability of the timely payment of interest and principal. Bonds are classified as short-term, medium term, and long-term:
• Short-term bonds mature in fewer than five years.
• Intermediate-term bonds mature between five and ten years.
• Long-term bonds mature in more than ten years.

---

1   This presentation will not include commodities or collectables as investments.

In general, shorter-term bonds have lower interest yields, less volatility, and are considered less risky than longer-term bonds. Correspondingly, longer-term bonds usually have higher interest yields, more volatility, and more risk.

Treasury bonds, those issued by the federal government, are considered the safest[2] investment available, and are often called the "gold standard."

Most municipal bonds are considered relatively safe investments, because if the revenues of their issuing entities fall short of expectations, the appropriate citizens can be taxed to make up the shortfall. Municipal bonds are desirable for individual investors, because their interest payments are not subject to federal income tax, and if the owner is a resident of the state in which the issuing entity exists, the bonds may not be subject to state or city taxes as well.

Corporate bonds are issued by corporations and are configured with a myriad of variables: maturities, interest rates, callability, exchange features, discounts, etc.

Other fixed-income instruments include savings accounts, certificates of deposit, and money market accounts.

Why Invest in Fixed-Income Instruments

In most instances, fixed-income instruments are best considered as a repository for wealth, a parking place for money that will soon be needed. Savings accounts, checking accounts, money-market funds, and CDs provide ready cash when needed. Their redemption value is fixed and their yields are fixed. Rarely does anyone lose money by having them.[3] In the case of savings accounts, your deposits are insured by the Federal Deposit Insurance Corporation (FDIC). The trade-off for this certainty is the low return on your investments. For short-term (one to five years) needs, fixed-income instruments make sense. For long-term investments, fixed-income instruments are subject to the ravages of inflation and in most cases should be avoided.

---

2 Safest in terms of payment of interest and principal, but except for some specific US Treasury obligations, there is no safety from inflation eating away at the principal.

3 However, if bonds are traded before maturity, a capital loss may occur.

24

Equities

Equities, also called stocks, represent ownership interests in corporations. For this discussion, we will limit ourselves to *common* stocks, which are the ones most likely to be of interest to you. There are thousands of corporations whose stocks are traded on established exchanges such as the New York Stock Exchange, or the Nasdaq. These stocks may be categorized in several ways:

1. Market Capitalization. Market capitalization indicates the value the market puts on a corporation. It can be computed by multiplying the number of shares outstanding by the current value of each share. Corporations can be classified as:
   - Large Capitalization (large-cap), meaning its shares are worth $10 billion or more, or
   - Medium Capitalization (mid-cap) meaning its shares are worth between $2 billion and $10 billion, or
   - Small Capitalization (small cap), meaning its shares are worth less than $2 billion.

2. Primary Appeal to Investors.
   - Value stocks are those that are selling cheaply, considering their present and future earnings. These stocks are expected to rise to better reflect their intrinsic value.
   - Growth stocks are those that are growing their sales and earnings faster than other stocks. This growth can be within an industry, or in the market at large.
   - Income stocks are those that presently and historically pay above average dividends. Investors buy these stocks for their income, and also to participate in growth in earnings of the corporation, which will be reflected in their prices, and probably as well in the increases in the dividends.

It should be noted that these categories—value, growth, and income—are not discrete. Rather, there is often some overlap. For instance, a growth stock could be selling at a bargain price, making it a value stock as well. It could also provide a decent dividend, making it an income stock too. So, in this classification scheme, the assignment of a label (value, growth, or income) indicates its primary appeal to investors, but not necessarily its only appeal.

The grid below shows how these two variables—size and investor objectives—can be graphed. This table could be used to classify domestic stocks, international stocks, single county stocks, or individual stocks within an industry. And portfolios (e.g. mutual funds) can be classified according to the same criteria.

	Large Cap	Mid Cap	Small Cap
Growth			
Income			
Value			

3. The Nature of Their Business. Corporations can be classified by their broad sector, and within the sector, by their industry, and finally by the name of the particular corporation. For example:
   - The Financial Sector includes the banking industry, and stocks such as Wells Fargo and Citibank.
   - The Healthcare Sector includes the drug industry, and stocks such as Pfizer and Actavis.
   - The Utilities Sector includes the electric utilities industry, and stocks such as Duke Power and Wisconsin Energy.

Price Variation between Stocks and Bonds

Stock prices of a corporation vary, sometimes considerably, over a period of time. Bond prices vary too, but usually not nearly as much as stock prices. That's because bondholders expect to get their investment back at a certain time, the maturity date. Stockholders may never get their investment back. For this reason, investments in bonds are considered generally safer than stocks.

Research on investment markets over a period of many decades shows that, taken collectively, investments in common stocks yield higher returns over time than investments in bonds. The important phrase here is "over time." In periods of recession such as the 1930s or the 1970s, stocks went nowhere, while bonds returned a steady income. On the other hand, in the expansionary environment of the 1960s and the 1990s, common stocks did much better than bonds. Then, in the first few years of the 21st century, bonds did better than stocks. Economic conditions change, and markets change. When planning for retirement, you are going to be a long-term investor, so the ups and downs of the stock market may not affect you in the long run.

The Upside and Downside of Bonds

There is some risk in owning bonds. They could <u>default</u>, meaning that the principal might not be paid at maturity, and/or the interest payments might not be paid in a timely manner. But the risk of default on investment grade[4] bonds is small. By owning bonds, you are trading off low risk of bonds for the reward of potential price appreciation available from stocks. This is a fair exchange.

However, there is a downside. If you hold long-term bonds (e.g. those maturing in 5, 10, or 20 years) to maturity, there is a significant risk of inflation. If a bond has a nominal yield of, say, 6% and the inflation rate as it matures is 3%, then your real (inflation adjusted) yield is 3%.

If long-term bonds are deemed appropriate for you, two types of U.S. government bonds may be suitable. One is Treasury Inflation-Protected Securities (TIPS), and the other is Series I Savings Bonds. As obligations of the U.S. Treasury, these bonds are considered to be risk-free as to timely payment of interest and principal. And both have protection against inflation. However, there are differences in liquidity, availability of face values, minimum purchase requirements as well as other characteristics.

Why Invest in Equities

Equities (stocks) represent ownership interests in businesses. Of course, the purpose of any corporate business is to make money for its owners, the stockholders. There is no more basic concept to free-market capitalism than this. So, why do I bring it up? Because fixed-income instruments cannot make the claim that they are making money. At best, they are repositories for wealth for their owners. They pay interest to the owners, and, in general, they do preserve wealth, although their value—interest and principal—are subject to the vagaries of inflation. Corporate fixed-income instruments are loans to businesses, which provide financing for <u>their</u> activities that make money. These instruments don't participate in the profits of the business, except to the extent that the interest and principal of the loans will be paid off by the profits.

---

4   Investment grade bonds are rated by Standard & Poors as AAA, AA, A, or B

And as for commodities (and also collectables), I don't consider them to be investments. They don't earn any money, and they don't pay any interest. They are purchased because their owners believe that their value will increase over time. Perhaps it will. But nonetheless, they are speculations, pure and simple.

For these reasons, equities are the best investment for the long-term. There are business cycles during which equities lose value, and then often gain it back (and then some). It is during the downward leg of the cycle that people can get discouraged. But history has shown that in the long run, investors are way ahead with equity investments, rather than the alternatives.

Staying Invested in Equities
We must keep a historical perspective on the stock market. If we don't, we can make serious errors of omission. We know that the economy and stock prices are always changing: there are good times and bad times, high points and low points. When there are bad economic times, some people turn pessimistic about the stock market, the economy, and life in general, and this negative outlook can distort their thinking. A good example of this can be found in the history of the United States in the last third of the 20th century.

From the mid-1960s through the 1970s there existed a period of great national unrest and turmoil. The country was engaged in an unpopular war in Viet Nam while great social change and civil disobedience were taking place at home. The White House was rocked by the Watergate scandal, the President resigned, the Vice-President copped a plea for some serious mischief and resigned, and the Attorney General of the United States, the chief law enforcement official in the nation, ended up in prison! Assassinations of national leaders took place. It was a bad, bad time.

And if that weren't enough there was the economy. It was in shambles. There was an Arab oil embargo, and a stagnant economy coupled with raging inflation, from which was developed the word *stagflation*. Economists were befuddled. It wasn't supposed to work this way. Fiscal and monetary policies didn't seem to be able to correct the situation. People in general were angry, scared, and doubtful as to whether our system of free market capitalism and indeed our form of government were sustainable. And many of these people extended their pessimism to a whole range of other issues.

In April 1966, the cover of *Time* magazine asked, "Is God Dead?" Three years later, the cover of the same magazine asked, "Is God Coming Back to Life?" Ten years later in 1979, the cover of *Business Week* magazine proclaimed, "The Death of Equities." In fact, twenty-five years later, also in unsettled economic times, I attended a workshop presented by an outfit that was selling a proprietary procedure that produced income through trading options. One of the first comments made by the presenter was, "Buy-and-hold is dead."

With regard to the statements regarding the deaths of equities and buy-and-hold investment strategies, perhaps someone should tell Warren Buffet. He seems to have done all right for himself and other investors in Berkshire Hathaway using a buy-and-hold strategy.

The life or death of God or even God's existence are matters of faith and cannot be argued with reason. But the ideas of the death of equities, and of the buy-and-hold investing principles, are disproved by history, and are clearly erroneous. These negative statements were made in a context of an unsettled economy and unsettled times, by shortsighted and short-term investors, who tend to be overly pessimistic in such times.

But long-term investors with a sense of history know better. In the mid-1970s, the Dow Jones Industrial Average was selling at about 700. As I write, it is over 15,000. At the same time, the S&P 500 was selling at about 100. Now, this benchmark is selling at over 1,700 and closing fast on 1,800. Some death!

Your Residence as an Investment

Many folks purchase a house[5] to reside in. They may stay in it for 20 or 30 years, have it fully paid off, and consider it a financial asset. In all probability, the house is worth more, perhaps much more than the original purchase price. This is all well and good. But converting the house to cash may present a problem.

Residential property is not considered a liquid asset. Its conversion to cash may depend upon the residential real estate market in which the

---

5   In this presentation, a "house" will also include a condominium or a cooperative apartment.

property is located. Now, markets go up and, as was realized by many people in 2008, markets can go down as well. Making money from the sale of your house is not a sure thing. The primary purpose of home ownership should be having a place to live. If, when you sell the house you make a profit, so much the better.

Typically, homeowners have to finance the purchase of their houses by taking out mortgage loans. And over the years, the loans may be paid down, and then they have clear and full ownership of the property. Because so much time has past since the house was purchased, and its value has increased so much, they may believe that the house was a great investment. From the point of view of having had the benefits of house ownership, it probably was a great investment. But considering it as a financial investment, maybe not so.

There has been research tracking the value of residential real estate over the 20th century. This was a time of increasing real estate value, but also a time of inflation. The findings of the research show that over most time periods, the value of residential real estate increases at about the rate of inflation. So rather than being a spectacularly profitable investment, it's more like a savings account in which deposits were made over the years, and in which interest was paid and compounded over a long period.

Chapter Five

Portfolio Investing

A key tenet of a conservative investment philosophy is diversification of assets. Sometimes, individual sectors, industries, and stocks decline in value. If the risk of this decline is spread over several sectors, industries, and stocks, often the loss from them may be offset by the gains in the others. Thus, it is prudent to aggregate a portfolio of stocks.[1]

Some people who have had some experience with investing in financial instruments build their own portfolios. Included in them might be cash, stocks, and bonds, and other financial instruments. Selecting and managing your own portfolio is an interesting but time-consuming activity. But if you're not careful, you could incur severe losses. However, for most investors, the easiest and most appropriate means to have a portfolio of financial instruments is to buy one already in existence. Mutual funds, closed-end funds, and exchange-traded funds (ETFs), represent already existing portfolios. Let's look at each of these investment vehicles.

Mutual Funds
When you buy shares of a mutual fund, you are buying shares of a portfolio of financial instruments. There are literally thousands of mutual funds available to you. Some contain largely equities, and some fixed-income. Some funds combine the two with varying proportions of each. These are called balanced funds. There are many variables that characterize specific mutual funds, and these will be discussed later in this chapter.

Closed-End Funds
The mutual funds just discussed are referred to as open-ended funds, because more shares are created when more money is invested. There is no limit to the number of shares that comprise a mutual fund. The shares are purchased and redeemed directly from the mutual fund itself. The price of the shares purchased or sold on a given day, is the closing price on the day of the transaction. This price represents the net asset value of the underlying portfolio.

---

1   This is true as well for asset classifications, e.g. stocks, bonds, real estate, cash, etc. This discussion will be limited to stocks because for most readers of this book, this will be the source of their wealth.

Closed-ended funds, however, are portfolios of financial assets that trade on a stock exchange. There are many fewer of these compared to mutual funds. Like other listed stocks, closed-end funds have a finite number of shares outstanding, and can be purchased from other investors who are selling their shares on the stock market. The price of the shares is determined by supply and demand, just as is the case for other stocks. The stocks of closed-end funds generally sell at a discount from their net asset values.

Exchange-Traded Funds (ETFs)

Exchange traded funds are a relative newcomer to the family of portfolio funds. They are similar to closed-end funds in some ways. They trade on stock exchanges and their prices are determined by supply and demand of the market. Most of them are index funds that focus on a particular class of assets, such as the S&P 500, high-dividend paying stocks, single country stocks, and others. They usually sell at or very near their net asset value.[2]

Proprietary funds

Many financial institutions maintain their own mutual funds and/or ETFs. Sometimes these funds under-perform non-proprietary funds of the same type so be careful to note management fees and sales charges compared to other similar funds. The advice provided may be free but you might pay for it in decreased returns.

In the following discussion, because each represents a portfolio of financial assets, all three of these investment vehicles—mutual funds, closed-end fund, and ETFs—will be considered collectively and be referred to as "funds."

What funds are appropriate for you? You need to think through your own particular situation and choose the ones that make sense. In other words, approach decision-making regarding investments in mutual funds in a deliberate, thorough, and linear fashion. There are two general questions to consider if investing in a fund.

Should you even invest in a fund? Consider your time horizon. Purchasing

---

2   This is because there are many traders (arbitrageurs) who carefully follow these indexes. When they see a discrepancy between the net asset value of the index and the trading price of the ETF, they will sell one and buy the other, making a profit on the spread between the two. Such activity keeps trading prices very close to, or at, the net asset value.

funds with stock portfolios should be thought of as long-term investments, at least three to five years out. If the money you're thinking of investing will be needed in less than five years, stay out of funds. Rather, put the money in a CD, short-term bonds (held to maturity), a savings account, or a money market account so as to maintain liquidity. If you invest in funds and you are going to need the money in, say, two or three years, it could very well happen that the value of your initial investment would be worth less than when you invested it. That's no fun.

What is your risk tolerance? This goes along with your time horizon. If the thought of possibly losing money really bothers you, be sure to stay with bond funds or big cap stock funds. If you are age 30 and you are investing for retirement, go with more stocks than bonds. If you make a bad choice at least you'll have time to make things right.

Having answered these three questions, your next decision is what kinds of funds to invest in. There are more than 8,000 mutual funds and similar investments from which to choose. My preference is to keep your portfolio simple. There are thousands of possible configurations. Here are three possibilities:
- 80% in a balanced domestic fund and 20% in an international stock fund.
- 60% in an S&P index fund, 20% in a small cap fund, and 20% in an international stock fund.
- 80% in a total stock market index fund, and 20% in a total international index fund.

Such portfolios cover the scope of domestic and international investing and provide a great deal of diversity. I recommend limiting your investments in funds to three, or perhaps four or five. My experience with clients is that those with more than a few funds end up in a bookkeeping nightmare. Monthly, quarterly, and annual statements are just the beginning. There are associated flyers, letters, directors' elections, etc. representing a plethora of paper that will crowd your mailbox, snail-mail and e-mail. And then there's tax time. And don't forget the record keeping. Follow the KISS principle (keep it simple, stupid).

Selecting a Fund
If you have decided that investments in funds are appropriate for you, there are a few major factors to consider before you make your selection.

Loads and Expenses

Be careful here. Loads (sales charges) and expenses can eat away at the value of your funds, and severely diminish the returns from your investments in funds.

First, avoid funds with sales charges. As a rule, they do no better than those without sales charges (no-load fund), and often do worse. Why? The payment of the sales charge reduces the amount of money actually invested. If you invest $10,000 in a fund with a 4% load, only $9,600 will be invested. In order for the fund to meet or exceed whatever benchmark it uses for comparison, it will first have to overcome the 4% loss of capital. This will entail taking greater risks than would be the case otherwise. On the other hand, if you will purchase a no-load fund, the entire $10,000 is invested. There are hundreds of no-load funds to choose from.

Second, watch out for high expense ratios. Some funds charge a sales load and some funds don't. But all funds charge a management fee for providing their services. These fees cover costs such as the managers' salaries, office overhead, marketing expenses, transaction costs, etc. and are stated as a percentage of the assets being managed. For example, Fund H has an expense ratio of 1.3%. That means that for every $100 of your investment, a management fee of $1.30 is being charged. So if you make a $10,000 investment in Fund H, $130 will be charged, and this percentage charge is made every year (unlike a sales charge), and the charge will be taken from the Fund's earnings. If the fund's investments yielded 7% in a given year, you would receive only 5.7% return. If the fund's investments had a negative yield of 4% in a given year, your actual loss would be 5.3%.

The cumulative effect of the management fees can add up over time, and can have a significant impact on your total return. For example, let's say you have $10,000 to invest and your choices are HiFee Fund and LoFee Fund, with management fees of 0.8% and 0.2% respectively. If both funds have the same 7% annual return for ten years, the HiFee fund will be worth $18,249 and the LoFee fund will be worth $19,307. Thus, you would have $1,058 more with the LoFee fund, representing a difference of 5.8%.

Let's look at a real life example. In 1995, Northern Small Cap Value

Stock Fund earned 27.7% and had a 1% expense ratio, making the effective yield 26.7%. Vanguard Small Cap Value Index earned 27.4% and had an expense ratio of 0.23%, making the effective yield 27.2%. These data are displayed in Table 5-1. The Vanguard fund with its lower expense ratio had a net yield that was higher than the Northern fund. Although the difference is only 0.77%, over time this can really add up and decrease the total return of the investor.

Table 5-1
Comparison of Two Small-Cap Value Funds

Fund	Nominal Yield	Expense Ratio	Net Yield
Northern	27.7%	1.00%	26.7%
Vanguard	27.4%	0.23%	27.2%
Difference	0.3%	0.77%	0.5%

Expense ratios vary considerably. Index funds such as Vanguard's S&P 500 generally have a low expense ratio: Vanguard's S&P 500 Index Fund's is 0.18%. That makes sense, since management of the fund is a no-brainer: the stocks in the S&P 500 are already picked, and all that needs to be done is to rebalance from time to time, and also modify the portfolio as some stocks fall off the index and are replaced by stocks new to the index. A typical managed (non-index) fund has an expense ratio of 1.3%. International funds' expense ratios run higher, typically 1.75%, probably because of the higher transaction cost associated with foreign investing.

Diversify your funds into different sectors of the market. There are funds for every sector, every market, every kind of equity or debt investments, and funds that combine these types. Invest in a few no-load low-expense funds that represent the world economy. The proportions of each fund will depend upon your individual circumstance.

When you've decided on which particular funds to buy, you want to focus on buying them right.

The Mechanics of Buying
Don't try to time the market. Everyone would like to invest when the market is low, and withdraw the investment when the market is high. Few, if any, people can manage to do that on a regular basis. Put in

the money into mutual funds over time, perhaps monthly deposits, and withdraw the funds over time as well. If you can, put in or take out the same dollar amount over time. This is the time-honored procedure known as dollar cost averaging and it really works.

But **do** time an initial deposit of funds. If you have a large amount of money to invest at one time, check carefully when the distributions of dividends and capital gains are made. This usually occurs once annually. The per share price of a mutual fund at any given time represents the value of its portfolio, including the dividends and capital gains it has taken in. If you buy into a mutual fund just before the annual distribution, you will be considered an owner as of that date. Accordingly, you will have to pay taxes on the distribution. The day after the distribution, the share value will probably decrease because of the distribution. If you buy a fund's shares right before the distribution, the value of your shares will go down and you'll have to pay taxes on the distribution. Therefore, if you have a large sum to invest in a mutual fund, be sure that you do it after the annual distribution date in order to avoid the double whammy of share value decrease and taxation of earnings.

And be careful about switching funds. Sometimes you really need to switch funds. For example, you have a diversity of funds that meets your goals but your goals change, or your time horizon changes, or you need to rebalance your portfolio of funds. If there is a good reason for switching funds, or for rebalancing the amount of money invested in particular sectors, then do it. But be careful. Even if you are in a no-load fund, if you switch out of it and you have a profit in it, you might have to pay taxes on the profits, whereas if you did not switch, the taxes would be deferred until you withdraw from the fund. And remember, styles of investing (growth, value, etc) change over time, and if you switch funds (sometimes called "chasing last year's yield"), you may be going from a fund whose time has come to a fund whose time has just passed. More on this later

Problems in Switching Funds

Many unsuccessful investors switch funds too frequently. Why is this a problem? Well, in the case of mutual funds that are sold through a brokerage house or an individual salesperson (financial advisor/planner/counselor), there is a sales charge (commission or load) of up to 5% that must be paid. If you buy $10,000 of Fund A with a load of 5%

only $9,500 ($10,000 minus $500) of your investment funds are actually invested, so you start off behind. Then, a year later, let's say Fund A (to keep it simple) didn't earn anything in dividends or capital gains, so you take the balance from Fund A, the $9,500, and invest it in Fund B instead, and pay another 5% load. This time the load is 5% of $9,500 or $475. Your loads for the two transactions are $500 and $450, a total of $950, and the amount of invested funds is now $9,050. If after the second year, there are still no dividend or earnings from Fund B, your $10,000 is now worth $9,050. To the degree that there were earnings from the fund, your loss will be less. If the fund lost money, then you're even in worse shape.

Common sense will tell you that paying sales charges multiple times will deplete the value of your investments significantly, and is a bad practice in which to engage. So, let's set aside the issue of sales charges.

The question is: why would you do this switching in the first place? There are several possible reasons.

Advisors' Incentives

If your financial advisor earns a commission or a sales fee on each sale of a fund, then he has an incentive to advise you to switch funds, perhaps frequently. This is called "churning." To my way of thinking, unless there is a really good reason for making a fund switch, it is a breach of ethical responsibility to advise someone to do so. An advisor without a sense of right or wrong, who is not looking out for you but rather for himself, is not the kind of financial advisor you want. Dump him.

Chasing Yields

Some people, of their own volition, switch funds too often because they are "chasing last year's yield." For example, let's say you own a fund that had a total return of 6.5% for the year. Then you pick up a financial magazine that touts on its cover something like, "Five of Last Year's Hottest Funds," and in the article are listed five funds that had total returns ranging from 11.3% to 19.9%. But your mutual fund returned only 6.5%. And you read this, give yourself a dope slap, and say to yourself, "What I jerk I am! I could have doubled my return if only I had been in that fund."[3]

---

3   As an aside, I believe that investors when speaking about their failures, should never use the phrases, I would have or I could have or I should have when referring to their investments of any kind: stocks, bonds, real estate, collectables, etc. Don't invite regret. Look forward, not backward.

The implication of the magazine article is that if you had invested in any of these funds, you would have done better than most investors, and as you look at your fund's return you nod your head sadly, because it may be true.

But don't beat yourself up about this. Hindsight is always 20/20, and Monday morning quarterbacks are infallible. Those of us who live in the real world, where we make predictions of returns based upon facts, logic, reasonable assumptions, and a knowledge of how markets work, are forward looking and can have reasonable expectations for success.

Should you switch to one of these funds? Not necessarily. There are two points to consider: the type of fund and the luck of the manager.

Switching Types of Fund

Let's consider the type of fund first. There are mutual funds for virtually every slice of the market: large cap, mid cap, small cap, international, developing countries, growth, value, blended, foreign bonds, domestic bonds, and varied combinations of these types. Some years ago, my friends at Citigroup/SmithBarney sent me a wonderful chart entitled "Annual Returns for Major Indices (1987-2006)." Each of ten indices, which reflect in large part the mutual fund types just mentioned, is ranked from 1 (highest return) to 10 (lowest return) for each year. Moreover, the ten indices are color-coded.

Just by observing the color-coding, I notice there are very few consistent patterns: it's unusual to see one color in the same rank over a period of years. Rather, there is a general tendency for the indices to shift in rank and actual returns from year to year. For example, in the year 2000 and 2001, small cap value stocks were ranked 1st in both years with returns of 22.8% and 14.0% respectively. In those same two years, emerging markets were ranked 10th and 5th with returns of –30.6% and –2.4%. In 2002, domestic bonds were 1st (11%) and emerging markets were ranked 3rd (-6.0%), while small cap value stocks were 4th (-11.45). In 2003, emerging markets were 1st (56.3%), small cap value were 4th (46%) and domestic bonds were 9th (4.7%). These data came from four contiguous years. If you were to skip around a bit, the changes would be even more dramatic.

What does this mean? It means that for any given year, investor sentiment and/or global macroeconomic factors influence which sectors of the market will do better than others on a relative basis, whether measured by rank or by total earnings. There are some generalities that can be made: in good times small stocks do best, and in bad times either bonds or large cap stocks do best. There may be some truth to that, but one should always remember the quotation of Justice Oliver Wendell Holmes: "No generality is worth a damn, including this one."

Why do I bring this up? Because when you chase last year's yield, you may very well be shifting from one type of fund to another, and the one you switch to may have had its run, whereas the one you switched from may be ready for its own advance. For example, if you owned a large cap growth fund in 2004 that yielded 6.3%, and you observed that for that same year, the small cap value fund yielded 22.3%, you might switch from the large cap growth to the small cap value. Unfortunately, for 2005 the large cap yielded 5.3%, and the small cap value yielded even less, 4.6%.

This kind of switching is a bit like market timing, the decision to own or not own stocks depending on where you think the market will be in the future. Neither is a good policy, and few investors are right on a regular basis.

Switching Within a Fund Type
Okay, you say. Switching to or from differing types of funds may be a bad idea. How about switching among the same type of funds, for example switching from a large cap growth fund to a different large cap growth fund? Of course, as a rational person, if you did this, you'd want to switch from a lower yielding fund to a higher yielding fund of the same type. Surely, this must be good, right?

Well, not necessarily. Let's look at this carefully. There exists a finite number of large cap growth stocks from which a selection can be made for inclusion into a portfolio. Well-trained and highly talented fund managers do qualitative and quantitative analyses of these stocks. Typically, the differences between the yields of two different funds selecting individual stocks from the same pool of stocks will be small in percentage terms, but if you make a large investment in one rather than the other, the dollar difference can be significant, and naturally you want the higher return. So, you switch from Fund A, the lower yielding fund, to Fund B, the higher yielding fund. Surely, that makes sense, doesn't it?

Not necessarily. If you do that switch, you are assuming that the manager of Fund B is more talented than that of Fund A. That may indeed be the case if Fund B consistently does better than Fund A. But that is rare. Here's another explanation: the manager of Fund B was luckier. Well, what's wrong with that? Legend has it that when Napoleon was asked what kind of generals he wanted to have, he said, "I want lucky ones." So, of course, go with the luckier manager. But not so fast!

The Role of Luck

Without getting too deeply in to metaphysics, let me ask, "Are some people luckier than others? Are there people who are born with the blessing of good luck, and others with the curse of bad luck?" Perhaps. But setting aside genetic health problems, who your parents were, and in what era and what country you were born in, I believe that luck is randomly distributed among people and given enough time it all equals out. You can have a lucky thing happen to you, and then you can have an unlucky thing happen.

Moreover, you can have a string of good luck and you can have a string of bad luck. But I believe that given enough time, we will all get our share of good and bad luck. My point is that for a given year (or other period), the Fund B manager, the more successful one, may be luckier than her Fund A counterpart, and it is her luck that makes her more successful, not necessarily her talent. And if my belief holds true, then the Fund A manager will have his place in the sun one of these days. So you need to ask yourself how you feel about luck.

Another way of looking at this issue is to consider the high returns of Fund B as an anomaly, an aberration, an outlier, which is unlikely to repeat itself any time soon. Most anomalies over time come back to normal. Statisticians refer to this as a reversion to the mean, and it's a phenomenon that is present in many fields.

Now, all this discussion assumes that there is a randomness to Fund B's high returns. But if indeed time after time, year after year, Fund B's return is higher than Fund A's return, maybe it's not randomness at all, but rather a talent that Fund B manager has and that Fund A's manager does not have. And of course, if that's the case you might reasonably be inclined to invest in Fund B.

The Role of Risk

Risk is somewhat related to luck. Whatever the investment, there is always a trade-off between risk and reward. Of course, if you want a high return, you'll need to take on some risk. And if you want to limit your risk, you'll have to settle for a potentially lower return. Portfolio managers generally seek to maximize the return for any given level of risk, or conversely, minimize the risk for any given level of return. Indeed, that's what they are paid to do.

But suppose a fund manager who is seeking to increase her fund's return takes on a good bit more risk than other fund managers. And further suppose that her fund's return in a given year was indeed higher than that of other funds. Was there too much risk taken on? That could account for the higher return. Or maybe she was just lucky. But bear in mind that rewards from risk, like luck, tend to revert to the mean. And if she consistently invests in risky portfolios to increase the return, unless she is very lucky or inordinately talented, sooner or later the risky chickens will come home to roost, and her higher returns will turn into lower returns, possibly even negative returns.

Chapter Six

The Benefits of Deferring Taxes

When Uncle Sam gives you a gift, open it, rejoice, and be glad in it. He gave us the opportunity to invest for our future retirement, and not pay taxes on the earnings while the money is accumulating, or in the case of a Roth IRA, never pay taxes on it. We should take advantage of this.

Tax Deferral

As a people, we Americans are taxed on our income at the federal level as well as sometimes at the state and local levels. Taxes are also applied to our investment income. Within recent memory, interest, dividends, and short-term capital gains[1] were taxed as regular income, subject to tax rates as high as 39.6%, while long-term capital gains[2] were taxed at a maximum as high as 20%. Beginning in 2001 and continuing to the end of the first decade of the 21st century, tax rates on many investments have been reduced, but still they represent a diminution of returns on investments.

However, Congress wants to encourage us to prepare financially for our retirement, so it has given us some gifts in the form of letting us defer, and sometimes even avoid entirely, the taxes which would normally be paid on the earnings from our investments. These gifts include employer sponsored retirement plans, such as traditional pension plans (defined benefit), 401(k) plans (defined contribution), Keogh and SEP-IRA plans for the self-employed, Individual Retirement Accounts of many types, and 403(b) plans for some employees working in the non-profit area.

Investment vehicles that allow tax-free compounding (i.e. tax payments deferred or avoided) are excellent opportunities for the enhanced accumulation of wealth. The differences between compounding in taxable accounts contrasted to compounding in non-taxable accounts are dramatic. For instance, assume you make payments of $100 at the beginning of every month to an account that yields a 6% return, and you are in the 30% marginal tax bracket. In a fully taxable account your balance in 20 years would be $37,513. However, in a non-taxable account, after 20 years your balance would be $46,204, a difference of $8,691.

---

1   Gains of the sale of assets held for less than one year.
2   Gains on the sale of asset held for a year or more.

Table 6-1 shows the results of making monthly investments of $100 for 20, 30, and 40 years of compounding at a rate of 6% when you are in a marginal tax bracket of 30%.

Table 6-1
Taxable vs. Tax Deferred Compounding of Earnings
Of $100 Invested Monthly

Years	Taxable	Tax Deferred	Difference
20	$37,513	$46,204	$8,691
30	71,934	100,452	28,518
40	124,280	199,149	78,869

As you can see from the Table 6-1, the benefits of investing in tax deferred accounts rather than taxable accounts are enormous. That's why investing in 401(k)s, 403(b)s, IRAs, and other tax-deferred accounts makes a lot of sense.

Taking Withdrawals from Tax-Favored Retirement Accounts
When Congress set up these tax favored investment accounts—401(k), 403(b), IRA, Roth IRA—it sought to encourage individuals to save for their retirement. Thus, there are rules that govern the withdrawals from these accounts. The rules are subject to change by Congress, or the Internal Revenue Service's interpretation, but here is the gist of the rules as of this writing in the fall of 2013.

Under current law, there is no penalty for taking withdrawals after age 59 ½. If you withdraw funds before that age, the withdrawal may be subject to a 10% penalty. In all these accounts except a Roth IRA, you must begin to take withdrawals, the required minimum distributions (RMDs), at age 70 ½. The penalty for a late withdrawal is 50% of the required withdrawal.

For a 401(k) or a 403(b), if you take withdrawals before age 59 ½, it is considered an early withdrawal, and there are stringent rules to follow. If you have a bona fide hardship (as defined by the IRS) such as un-reimbursed medical expenses, or a disability, there will be no penalty assessed.

With an IRA, if you want to use the funds for the first time purchase of a residence or for educational expenses, you may borrow the money for these purposes, and there will be no penalty assessed. To my way of thinking, perhaps the worst penalty for early withdrawal of these funds is the loss of the principal withdrawn, and the loss of the earnings on that principal that might have been. Thus, I discourage early withdrawals unless absolutely necessary.

Planning for Supplemental Retirement Income
In Chapter Three, you saw the miraculous effects of compounding on a relatively small amount of money, over a period of time. You can use this technique to develop a substantial addition to your retirement funding through systematic contributions to non-tax-advantaged accounts. Here's how this can happen.

Let's say you're 30 years old, and you plan to retire at age 65. So, you have 35 years of time for compounding until retirement. Further, you plan on living another 35 years until age 100. And let's say that you want to have a corpus of $300,000 to draw upon at the time of your retirement. And finally, let's assume that you'll be investing prudently, making regular monthly investments, and receive a return of 6% compounded monthly. Here's how it would play out.

Table 6-2
Funding a Target Amount of $300,000 Over 35 Years

Monthly Payments	$211
Annualized	$2,532
Total Paid in Over 35 Year	$88,620
Value of Account After 35 Years	$300,000

As shown in Table 6-2, you would need to contribute $211 monthly, for an annual contribution of $2,532. Your total contribution over the 35 years would be $88,620. And now, at age 65, you have $300,000 to draw from.

Assuming you plan to live another 35 years to age 100, How much can you take out each month as supplemental retirement income? More than you might expect.

Table 6-3
Distributions From a $300,000 Principal Over 35 Years

Monthly Payments Received	$1,771
Annualized	$20,532
Total Paid Out Over 35 Year	$718,620
Balance at the End of 35 Years	0

As shown in Table 6-3, from this $300,000 principal you would draw $1,771 monthly, for an annual withdrawal of $20,532. Your total withdrawal over the 35 years would be $718,620. After 35 years of withdrawals, the entire account would be depleted.

So, you made monthly contributions of $211 over 35 years, and then you withdrew monthly payouts of $1,771 for 35 years. How could this happen?

This is the magic of compounding. As you make the monthly contributions of $211 over 35 years, the earnings compound month after month, year after year, and the result is $300,000 from which you can draw. When you start your monthly withdrawals of $1,771, from the $300,000 corpus, the balance left in the account continues to earn interest.

As another example, if you wanted to have a target amount of $500,000 at retirement age, Tables 6-4 and 6-5 show how that works.

Table 6-4
Funding a Target Amount of $500,000 over 35 Years

Monthly Payments	$351
Annualized	$4,212
Total Paid in Over 35 Year	$147,420
Value of Account After 35 Years	$500,000

As shown in Table 6-4, you would need to contribute $351 monthly, for an annual contribution of $4,212. Your total contribution over the 35 years would be $147,420. And now, at age 65, you have $500,000 to draw from.

Table 6-5
Distributions From a $500,000 Principal Over 35 Years

Monthly Payments Received	$2,851
Annualized	$34,212
Total Paid Out Over 35 Year	$1,197,420
Balance at End of 35 Years	0

As shown in Table 6-5, from this $500,000 principal, you would draw $2,851 monthly, for an annual withdrawal of $34,212. Your total withdrawal over the 35 years would be $1,197,420. After 35 years of withdrawals, the entire account would be depleted.

A Real Example

The examples above are based on hypothetical situations. Here's a real life example of the effect of the early investing of a very small sum over a long period of time and letting it sit there to compound. The process of making systematic payments to an account, from which you intend to make later withdrawals, is called *funding an annuity*.

Time: 1973 to 1983
Amount invested: $30 per month for nine months of each of ten years: $270 per year. No further investments made after 1983.
Total amount invested: $2,700
Investment vehicles: 50% fixed income fund, 50% common stock fund. Earnings compounded tax-free.
Value on June 1, 2000: $51,932

Table 6-6
Example of Funding an Annuity

Monthly Payments	$30
Annualized (Nine-Month Year)	$270
Total Paid in Over 35 Year	$2,700
Years of Compounding After 10 Year Period	17
Account Value in Year 2000	$51,932

This example in Table 6-6 shows that even very small amounts can compound into sizable chucks of cash given enough years.

Table 6-7
Monthly Annuities from $51,932 Principal
Over Expected Longevity at Age 65

Monthly Payments Received	$280-305
Annualized	$3,360-$3,660

The investor in this example decided, at age 65, to begin to drawing on this amount, and decided rather than take the money in a lump sum, to have it annuitized[3], and receive instead, monthly payments of about $300, as shown in Table 6-7.

This is beautiful. He invested that $270 per <u>year</u> for ten years, and now receives even more, $300 per <u>month</u> for the rest of his life.

This real life example leads us into a presentation of annuities.

Annuities

In common parlance, an annuity is a payment made to you by an insurance company. You give the company a sum of money in one lump sum. Or, you can give the money bit by bit, as monthly payments over a period of years. This is referred to as the *accumulation phase* of an annuity. The company will invest your money, and at a predetermined date, usually age 65, will make monthly payments to you for the rest of your life. This is referred to as the *liquidation* or *distribution phase*.

The amount of the payment may be a set amount, known as a *fixed annuity*. Or, it might be different amounts in different years. This is known as a *variable annuity*. The details on these accounts will differ from company to company, and will depend on such factors as your age at the payout time, your expected longevity, the prevailing interest rate at the time of the initial payment you make, and a myriad of other factors.

But let's back up a moment. Strictly speaking, the term *annuity* is short for an *annuity contract*. When you enter into an annuity contract with an insurance company, you agree to give them money at a given time, and they agree to distribute money to you at a later date. The money is

---

3   An annuity is a monthly payment based on an amount of principal which payment can be paid for the duration of a person's life. The annuity in this example was in a supplemental retirement account, and was invested with an insurance company.

48

no longer yours. It belongs to the insurance company. They have the money, and you have their promise to distribute it to you later. That's the contract.

There are benefits to having an annuity contract.
- It disciplines you to put money away for retirement.
- The money compounds on a tax-deferred basis.
- It distributes money to you at regular monthly intervals, so you can't blow the whole investment on a whim.
- It is often combined with a life insurance policy to give added protection to your wealth.

But there are drawbacks as well.
- The money is distributed to you whether you want it or not, and only in amounts agreed to by the contract.
- Your investment in the annuity is not your money, it's the company's.
- There are expenses involved in maintaining your account, for which you will be charged.
- Also, there is often a hefty sales charge, which is taken from your investment right away.

Annuities are right for some people, and inappropriate for others. I don't necessarily endorse them or discourage people from buying them. Whether it's right for you or not will depend on many personal and idiosyncratic characteristics, and the totality of your balance sheet.

An Annuity-Like Program
You can take the concept of an annuity contract with an insurance company, and apply it in what I call a do-it-yourself annuity. If you have the discipline to do this, it can be a lot cheaper and equally as effective as most annuity contracts with insurance companies. Here's the way it might work.

Go back to Table 6-4. As shown, you contribute $351 monthly for 35 years to an account yielding 6% compounded monthly, you would have an account balance or $500,000. Table 6-5 shows how you can make monthly withdrawals of $2,851 for 35 years to deplete the account.

This is a do-it-yourself annuity. It saves a considerable amount of money in sales and administrative costs to do it this way, in contrast to an annuity contract with an insurance company. However, there are two facts of which you must be aware.

- Unless this account is in a 403(b) account or other tax-advantaged account such as an annuity offered by an insurance company, you will be required to pay taxes on all earnings, whether dividends, interest, or capital gains, in the year when you receive them.
- Also, inflation over the 70 years of these contributions and withdrawals will have eroded the purchasing power of the money in question.

On the positive side, however, there are advantages to doing it yourself.

- The money invested remains yours, not the insurance company's.
- If you die prematurely, the money will be part of your estate, and may be bequeathed to your heirs.
- You can take as much, or as little, from the account at any given time, rather than receive monthly payments from the insurance annuity.

Chapter Seven

Designated Retirement Plans

Many employers include in their employees' wage packages a contribution to a retirement plan of some sort. This can be an important fringe benefit in any job, and if funded and invested appropriately, this can be a key component of retirement income. There are two major types of retirement benefits sponsored by employers: defined benefit programs, and defined contribution programs.

Defined Benefit Plans

Years ago, many employers provided pension benefits for their employees. The employee made a contribution, the employer made a contribution, and the money went into a pension fund. At retirement, a formula was applied which used three factors:

- Number of years or service,
- Average salary of last several years,
- A given percentage.

These factors were multiplied together, and the product was a dollar amount from which an actuarially sound pension could be derived. This is the defined benefit, the annual pension that would be paid to the employee in monthly installments for the rest of his or her life. For example, Employee Jake worked for Acme Steel for 32 years, his average salary for the last five years was $75,000 and the percentage applied was 1½%. Multiplying the factors, 32 years times $75,000 times 1.5%, resulted in an annual benefit of $36,000 probably paid in monthly checks of $3,000. [1]

If your employer sponsors a defined benefit program, you will probably have no choice as to whether or not to participate. You're in it. Your contributions are pooled with those of others, and after a period of years, perhaps ten or so, you will be "vested." This means that you can leave the funds with the pension fund even if you no longer work for that employer, and when you get to a certain age, usually 65, benefits will be paid to you. If you leave before the vesting period, your contributions,

---

[1] Plans vary as to what constitutes years of service, how many years of salary go into computation of an average salary, and the specific percentage applied.

but not those of your employer, may be returned to you. Typically, you have no control as to where the pension funds are invested.

These defined benefit plans are sometimes called "old-fashioned pensions." Many state and municipal employees are covered by such pension plans. However, many private companies have phased them out (if they ever had them), and offer instead defined contribution plans.

Defined Contribution Plans/401 (k) Plans

These plans are known as 401(k) plans, after the section of the tax code where they appear. In defined contribution plans, employees make contributions representing a percentage of their salaries, perhaps 6%. Employers make a matching contribution, usually about half of the employees' but sometimes more.[2] The money goes into any of several possible investment vehicles under the supervision of a fiduciary institution.

Often the employee has a choice of which particular investments the money is put in. If you have a choice as to what asset types your account is invested in, choose a combination of 65% stock index funds, 20% international funds, 15% bond funds. The characteristics of these funds were discussed in prior chapters. As you get closer to retirement, you might change these percentages to be somewhat more conservative, depending on your overall financial situation. At retirement, the money in the employee's account may be withdrawn in a lump sum, or may be annuitized, thus yielding a monthly income.

Some employees who work for non-profit companies, such as hospitals and schools, are eligible for 403(b) plans, which work similarly to 401(k) plans. These are often the primary retirement plans for them. However, some state and municipal employees who are participants in their defined benefit programs may also have a supplemental 403(b) plan to enhance their retirement income. This supplemental plan is typically funded with only the employee's pre-tax money, and not the employer's.

Earnings on these accounts are tax-deferred, which means that the earnings can compound at a faster rate than if they were taxed annually. Generally, they are a good deal for you.

---

2   In these plans, as was the case with defined benefit plans, the details will vary from employer to employer.

If your employer offers a defined contribution program, you should participate in it. This is especially so if the employer offers a matching contribution. For example, if in a given year, you contribute $1,000, your employer might match half of that, $500. This employer $500 contribution represents a 100% yield on $500 of the $1,000 you contributed. That kind of return is hard to get anywhere and it's free. So, your $1,000 contribution is now worth $1,500. There's no risk on your part. Not bad!

Employer's Corporate Stock

Some corporations will make contributions to their employees' retirement plans with stock in the corporation, or options to buy the stock, often at a discounted price. If that is your only choice, take it, especially if it's free. But bear in mind that if that stock is the only security in your retirement plan, you may be sitting on a non-diversified portfolio, and this is dangerous. Should the company get into financial trouble, the value of your stock could be severely and negatively impacted. (Think Enron here.) And, on top of that, you might lose your job, a double whammy.

Some corporations will give their stock or stock options to employees' retirement systems, and then require the stock to be held for a certain period of time before it can be sold. If that is the case, then hold the stock, and when the mandatory holding period is over, consider whether you should continue to hold it. Even if the company is a good one, and you would like to retain ownership of your shares, bear in mind that your retirement fund lacks diversity. I'd recommend that you sell at least a portion of the stock, and reinvest the proceeds in other financial instruments. It's not good to take chances with your retirement funds.

Individual Retirement Accounts

Regardless of whether or not you have an employer sponsored retirement account, you may choose to have an Individual Retirement Account (IRA). Congress legislated IRAs in the early 1980s to encourage workers to take some personal responsibility for their retirement. Earnings in an IRA are tax-deferred until withdrawal. If you have a Roth IRA, the earnings in your account are tax-exempt, that is, you pay no taxes on any withdrawal after age 59 ½. There are income limits for starting a Roth IRA. For 2013, the income limits are $178,000 for a married couple, and $112,000 for a single person. If your modified adjusted gross income is more than this, you are not eligible to start a Roth IRA, but you still can contribute to a traditional IRA.

IRAs are funded by individuals with after-tax money.[3] The money must be "earned," that is, not money received from dividends or interest, so-called unearned income. The funds are held in an account clearly labeled with your name and *IRA*, in a fiduciary entity such as a bank, mutual fund, or brokerage house, which serves as the custodian of the account. There are limits as to how much you can contribute to an IRA. Under current law, for a traditional IRA, the maximum annual contribution is $5,500, or $6,500 if age 50 or older. For a Roth IRA, the same limits are imposed, except that if your Adjusted Gross Income is more than $110,000, the maximums are reduced and then become zero.

Funds in an IRA can be invested in a variety of financial assets such as bank accounts, CDs, mutual funds. If you want to manage the funds yourself, you may have a self-directed IRA at a brokerage house and buy financial assets yourself, or with the assistance of an advisor. There are some restrictions on the type of assets that may be held in an IRA. For example, collectibles and life insurance are not permitted. In addition, custodians of the IRA may place additional restrictions.

Care should be taken in deciding what assets are suitable for an IRA. For example, annuities are less desirable than other assets because their tax-advantaged characteristics are duplicated by those of an IRA. In contrast, assets that yield taxable dividends and/or interest (e.g. dividend-paying stocks, or interest bearing bonds) are appropriate because their earnings are tax-deferred or tax-exempt.

Withdrawals from an IRA may be made at any time without penalty after age 59 ½, and must be made after age 70 ½ or you will assessed a stiff penalty. Bear in mind that IRAs are funded independently of other retirement accounts, such as defined benefit or defined contribution plans. They are supplemental to these plans, and if funded well over a period of years, they can develop significant value, which can be tapped for retirement income.

Taxation of IRAs and 401(k)s

Traditional IRAs, funded with after-tax earnings, are subject to Required Minimum Distributions (RMDs) every year, starting at age 70 ½, and are based upon the December 31 balance of the previous year. The amount of the distributions is based on IRS life expectancy tables.[4] If you have

---

3   In the case of IRAs which allow a deduction for the contribution, before-tax money is used.
4   RMD tables are shown in Appendix B.

more than one traditional IRA, take all of the last year's December 31 balances, add them up, and apply that sum to the Tables. You make take your distribution from any or all IRA accounts, so long as the RMD is met. For tax purposes, subtract the amount you contributed to them (your basis) from the distribution. The remainder of the distribution will be taxed at regular income tax rates, regardless of whether the earnings were from dividends, interest, or capital gains.

Roth IRAs, also funded with after-tax earnings, are not subject to RMD rules, and when withdrawn are not taxable.

Traditional 401(k)s follow the same rules as the traditional IRAs, except that if you are still working, you don't have to take an RMD until you stop working. Unlike the IRA rules, if you have more than one 401(k), an RMD must be taken from each 401(k) separately. The 401(k)s may not be combined. [Why? Hey, I don't write the rules. I just pass them on!]

Roth 401(k)s have two separate accounts, one for the employee's contribution (funded with after- tax contributions), and one for the employer's contributions (funded with before-tax contributions). If you want to minimize the amount required to be withdrawn, at retirement you can roll over the employee's account to a Roth IRA. Then, only the employer's account will be subject to RMD rules.

Social Security

Many employees, both in the public and private sectors, are covered by Social Security (SS). This program was started in the Great Depression, and was aimed at providing some funds for retirees through a payroll deduction from those who are currently working. Presently, you pay 6.2% of your salary up to a wage base limit ($113,700 for 2013). Your employer pays the same amount.[5] This goes into a "trust fund."

The SS program presents a dilemma for potential beneficiaries. It is not now, and never was, an actuarially sound program. And notwithstanding the "trust fund" idea, there are not sufficient funds to provide currently projected promised benefits for all future retirees. Furthermore, you have no property rights to your anticipated SS benefit. In other words, it is not your money, and you won't get any of it until they give it to you.

---

5   An additional 1.45% for Medicare is also paid by you, with your employer kicking in a like amount. Currently, there is no wage base cap on this though.

Congress created the program in 1935. They have changed it many, many times, and could, and probably will, change it again. You will probably get some benefits, but those benefits will probably not be as generous as the benefits today's retirees are currently receiving. See Chapter Eleven for a discussion of taxation of SS benefits.

Chapter Eight

Protect Yourself

Most readers of this book probably have a measure of wealth already. Some will have more than others, but nevertheless this wealth will probably be an important start to a secure retirement. Your wealth, tangible and intangible, must be protected. This chapter will explore the various events that can threaten your wealth, and make recommendations for protecting it. The two topics are *insurance* and *estate planning*.

Insurance

Insurance, conceptually, is the transfer of risk from one party to another. For example, if you own a car, the value of that car could be diminished in a nanosecond if an accident were to occur, totaling your car. Without insurance, you're out the value of the car. That's the risk you took when you bought the car and drove it around. When you bought insurance, however, you transferred that risk to the insurance company. You paid them a premium to accept this transfer of risk, and the insurance company is to foot the bill for your vehicular mishap. This concept of transfer of risk applies to all insurance of any type.

For many employees, especially those employed by large firms, some insurance coverage is part of a package of fringe benefits. Employers purchase group policies that are relatively inexpensive, and generally have decent coverage. If you work for such an employer, that's wonderful. But if you don't, insurance coverage is something you need to take care of on your own.

Insurance for You

Insurance is a way of protecting yourself from financial calamity. Your insurance needs will vary according to your age, family situation, debt, and the amount of your wealth.

Life Insurance

You need life insurance in case of your unexpected death, when your net assets would not cover your financial obligations. For example, you need life insurance:

- if there are people who rely upon your income for their economic well-being, such people as your spouse or your children.
- if you have large amounts of debt, such as a mortgage loan, that would need to be paid off, so your family could continue to reside in your house.

The most appropriate life insurance for you, at this time in your life, is *term insurance*. This is insurance in its simplest form. You pay a monthly premium, and if you die, your beneficiaries are paid the face amount of the policy. Depending on the policy, the premium may increase every year, or it may be level for five or ten years, after which it will be raised for the next five or ten years. This is pure protection; there is no cash value to this policy, except of course, the payment of the face value amount that will occur upon your death.

For a non-smoking young adult, the cost of $100,000, $500,000 or even $1,000,000 coverage is not very expensive. Term life insurance is a commodity, with very small differences between policies. Buy it from a low-cost company with a solid financial rating. Quotes are available online.

Aside from protection of income in case of an early demise, life insurance can be an important component of estate planning. If the proceeds from a life insurance policy are paid directly to the beneficiary (not the estate of the deceased), no income tax needs to be paid by the recipient. This provides instant liquidity for the settlement of debts, and ready cash, which could be used while a will is probated.

Disability Insurance

In your pre-retirement years, it is more likely that you might become disabled rather than die. For this reason, disability insurance is something to consider. I recommend it. The cost of disability insurance will be determined by the age, sex, and occupation of the applicant. For example, an office worker will pay less for this insurance than a construction worker. Quotes are available on-line.

Car Insurance

Your insurance policy has set limits as to how much the company will pay for various events. If you have some wealth, and you find yourself in a situation where a judgment against you exceeds your insurance coverage, a plaintiff can go after your wealth to recover the balance of the judgment. So, bear this in mind when setting policy limitations.

In anticipation of the unlikely but possible scenario in which a judgment is rendered against you which exceeds the limits of your liability insurance, you can protect yourself with a Personal Umbrella Policy (PUP). A PUP is not very expensive, usually about $200. This will give you liability protection up to $1 million.

Health Insurance

Health costs in our country can be very expensive. If you have low income, and no assets, you may be eligible for Medicaid. The threshold for eligibility for this program varies from state to state. And, of course, for those over age 65, Medicare Part A is available at no cost. The issue of universal health insurance came to a head in 2010 with the passage of the Affordable Care Act (Obamacare), which will be implemented starting in 2013.

Presently, health insurance for many people is often provided by employers as a benefit, and by Medicare and Medicaid. Beyond those payers, people must get their insurance through private insurance companies. But many people don't. There are an estimated 50 million citizens who are not covered by health insurance. They are vulnerable, and if you are one of these people, your assets, your wealth, and of course, your health are all in jeopardy. The provisions of the Affordable Care Act may help to ameliorate this problem.

The Complexity of the System

I continue to be amused that the first time I walk into a doctor's office, the first question I'm asked is, "What insurance do you have?" Not what medical problems I have, not who referred me, just a question that goes right to the issue, "If we provide services to you, who is going to pay us?"

Understand that medical care, insurance, governmental and private responsibility, are complex issues. The rates and fees set by the medical establishment, doctors and hospitals, assume that the costs will be borne by the insurance companies or a governmental agency. What the medical service providers actually receive from these payers depends upon their arrangements with them.

Naked Is Not Good

If you are living your life without health insurance, you are said to be *going naked*. In the case of a medical need without insurance, hospitals are required by law to treat you in their emergency room. But, if you have assets, you may be charged for their services, and it is not cheap. In fact, a goodly number of personal bankruptcies are the result of unpaid doctor or hospital bills. This is a situation you want to avoid. When the Affordable Care Act is fully implemented, the potential damage to your personal wealth will be mitigated,

Long-Term-Care Insurance

As a person plans his or her retirement, one of the most difficult decisions to make is whether or not to have a long-term-care (LTC) insurance policy. In contrast, a decision about life insurance is fairly straightforward: you know you are going to die sooner or later, so figure out how much protection (if any) you need and how to structure it. Similarly straightforward is automobile insurance: look at the value of your car, how much liability protection you need, how much of a deductible can you bear. And in both cases, when a decision is made, seek the best value for the coverage you need.

It's not so simple with LTC insurance. First, you may die suddenly by natural or un-natural causes and never have a need for LTC. Second, LTC insurance can be very expensive especially if the premiums start late in life. Third, if you do indeed need LTC, it may not be for a long time, and you do not know what your personal or financial situation will be at the time that you might need it.

Why might you consider purchasing LTC insurance? Perhaps you don't want to dissipate your wealth on extended care if it is needed. Perhaps you don't want to burden your children with the obligation, financial and emotional, of providing for you in your old age. Or perhaps you have no children. Or perhaps you want a higher quality of care that could be purchased through LTC insurance rather than what governmental or social services agencies might provide. Or perhaps it's a combination of any or all of these factors.

Is Long Term Care Insurance Right for You?

Everything in life involves a trade-off of some sort, and a decision as to whether or not to purchase LTC insurance is no exception. There are many factors to consider as you ponder whether you should or shouldn't have this protection.

- <u>How old are you now?</u> If you are presently in your 60s or 70s, the cost of premiums for an individual is going to be in the neighborhood of $3,000 to $4,000, annually and can be expected to rise, as you get older. On the other hand, if you are in your 40s or 50s, the premiums will be lower, but you'll be paying them for a long time. Many people pay premiums for a while and then when the premiums get too high, they abandon their policies, forfeiting most of the premiums paid. Policies that are "guaranteed renewable" may be just that, but are not necessarily guaranteed renewable at the same premium you have been paying.
- <u>What are the chances that you might need it?</u> How long do you expect to live? How long did your ancestors live? What is your life-style compared to theirs? Are there any hereditary conditions that might affect your health and/or longevity?

Then there are the specific provisions of a given policy:

- <u>Would you want coverage care in your home and/or adult day care, as well as nursing home coverage?</u> Insurance coverage can vary and is priced accordingly.
- <u>What does nursing home care cost in your area?</u> This varies according to location. The nationwide median cost for a private room is about $230 per day. In the Atlanta area, a private room averages $180-200 per day.
- <u>Would you want coverage from day one when you need it, or could you do with a 30, 60, or 90-day elimination period before benefits kick in?</u> Coverage from day one is, of course, more expensive. The longer the elimination period (the period without coverage that precedes the covered period), the lower the premium. Think of it as analogous to a deductible on your car insurance. How much of an elimination period could you afford?
- <u>How long a period should you be insured for?</u> The average nursing home resident is there about two and a half years. Some last longer, some are there briefly.

If LTC Insurance Is Right for You, What Are Some Other Considerations?

1. Remember the adage, "Insurance is sold, not bought." In general, this is true. There are insurance salespersons, who will sell their products and will be paid commissions for their efforts, and this is how it should be. However, if you have already decided that you want to consider the purchase of a LTC policy, then look for a policy that you can buy independently. In other words, seek an insurer that has no sales force but rather offers policies directly to customers.

2. Look for a quality, reputable insurer. You may not need LTC for a long time, and you want to be sure that the insurance company will still around when you need it. A known name in insurance may cost a bit more but is probably worth it. Insurance companies are rated by Best, Standard & Poors, and Moody's.

3. Study different policies and observe their similarities and differences. Policies can be structured in many different ways, so decide on what you want and see what different insurers offer.

4. If you are young when you initiate a policy, see if inflation protection is available. It's a worthwhile option.

So, What To Do?

Should you, or should you not have LTC insurance? That is a very personal decision and depends on a myriad of factors relating to your health, wealth, risk tolerance, and family situation, as well as other factors.

Would your anticipated wealth and cash flow at retirement be such that you could finance long-term care by yourself? This is a major consideration in deciding whether or not to have LTC.

I can't give any general advice except for the following: Whatever you decide, be sure it's a family decision, because the decision will affect not just you. Also, bear in mind that Medicare does not have a provision for LTC, whereas Medicaid does. Thus, if you don't have LTC insurance, but then need LTC and have to pay for it yourself, when you have gone through your assets, Medicaid will pick up the tab, although the benefits are not particularly generous. Indeed, some people place their assets in an irrevocable trust known as a "Medicaid trust," in order to remove the assets from their ownership, and having done so, become eligible for Medicaid. Recently, Congress changed the Medicaid rules to include a "five year look-back" provision, which requires the trust to have been established at least five years before eligibility for benefits.

Protecting Your Estate
Part of protecting yourself while at and during retirement is protecting your assets when you no longer are able to manage them. This could be when you are mentally incapacitated, or perhaps when you die.

Your Will
If you haven't updated your will in the last five years, it would be good to take a look at it. You want to be sure that it reflects your current wishes for the disposition of your estate upon your death. While you're at it, look over your IRAs, 401(k)s, and insurance policies to ensure the current beneficiaries are who you want them to be. If you have minor children or grandchildren for whom you are responsible, be sure to make provision for their guardianship in case you cannot perform this function.

Asset Management
As part of the estate planning process, you should have a durable power of attorney for asset management drawn up. This document will allow a person designated by you to act in your stead, if you were to become physically or mentally incapacitated, and thus unable to handle your personal finances. Without such a document, the responsibility might very well go to someone who is not competent in this area. If this were the case, a local court might have to appoint someone to manage and/or administer your assets. I believe that you would prefer to name someone to deal with these matters rather than have that decision made by a court.

Health Management
You should also have a living will drawn up which includes a durable power of attorney for health care. A living will allows you to state your wishes as to the desired medical treatment at the end of your life, in the event that you become terminally ill or injured, and are incapable of stating your desires for treatment (or lack thereof) at that time. You may state what you do or do not want done to you if you are unable to communicate. A durable power of attorney for health care can be set up to be "springing," that is, to spring into operation at the time you become incapacitated.

Protecting Yourself from Malefactors

In this chapter, we have discussed ways to protect your assets—your money and your life—from various events that can have a negative effect upon them. So, we've dealt with life, disability, liability, and health insurance. Finally, we discussed end of life issues such as estate planning and long-term health care. However, beyond these events, you should also protect yourself from those people who make their living separating other people from their money.

One of my favorite financial jokes goes like this: Two people meet, one has money and the other has experience. When they leave each other, the one with experience has the money, and the one who had the money has the experience.

The human imagination knows no boundaries when those who love money plot to get it in nefarious ways. Chapter Twelve includes stories of two major malefactors you are probably already aware of. In Appendix C entitled "Fraud, Deceit, and Other Mischief," I extend the information by describing some ongoing approaches used by con artists.

Chapter Nine

At and Beyond Retirement

Near or at retirement, or shortly thereafter, you'll need to conduct a re-evaluation of your financial situation. The questions you asked and answered as part of your pre-retirement planning in Chapter One will need to be revisited and updated with new and current information.

1. Do you really want to retire?
If you enjoy your occupation and it is not too taxing upon you physically and/or mentally, you might want to stay in the workforce. But if you do indeed want to retire because you're tired of your job, or you want to spend more time with your grandchildren, or you want to play more golf, and you can afford not to work and still have sufficient income to meet your goals, then of course, do it.

2. What is the current status of your wealth?
You'll need to develop an updated balance sheet to know your current financial status.

3. What is your anticipated cash flow?
At this point, the sources and amounts of income in retirement should be known to you. You can probably anticipate what your cash outflow will be. Will your income be enough to sustain your desired lifestyle? Will you need to supplement your retirement income with part-time work?

4. What is your anticipated longevity?
You've made it this far. Considering the status of your health and the longevity of your ancestors, how much longer do you think you have to live?

In consideration of all these factors, you will be able to plan for financing your retirement. If you've invested your discretionary income wisely over the years, and done other appropriate planning, you should be in pretty good shape.

Before determining how much of your wealth to tap for purposes of financing your retirement, you need to make an important decision: Do you want to use all of your wealth on your retirement, leaving little to your heirs when you die? Or rather, would you like to have a comfortable retirement, but be assured that when you die there will be some decent money left for your heirs to inherit?

This is a major consideration, because it will influence the amount of money withdrawn from your wealth. You could decide to use it all, principal and earnings. Or you could decide to spend just the earnings from this wealth without invading the principal. Or, perhaps, you could decide on something in between.

Case Studies of Couples at Retirement

In order to enhance understanding of the planning process at the point of retirement, we'll look at two couples with differing levels of wealth. Most of the same questions must be asked, but the answers for each couple will be different.

Mel and Anita Cooper

Let's look at Mel and Anita Cooper, a fictional couple, who are each age 67, and have decided they really want to retire. They have two children, and three grandchildren. They own their house, free and clear, and expect to live in it for the rest of their lives. They are in good health, and they expect to live well into their 90s.

Take a look at their balance sheet. After a lifetime of living within their means, investing conservatively, and making good use of the tax benefits of retirement funds, they have amassed enough wealth to retire comfortably. Their financial asset base is over $1 million. Their liabilities are negligible. Financially, they are in great shape.

They decide to live on $120,000 annually while in retirement. They expect to receive Social Security benefits of $42,196. This leaves a shortfall of $77,804 that will be made up by tapping their financial assets. This will work. With financial assets of $1,271,201 and assuming a 6% growth rate, the annual withdrawal of $84,275 will more than cover the shortfall.

Figure 9-1
Mel and Anita Cooper - Balance Sheet, March 18, 2014
(All assets and liabilities are held jointly unless otherwise specified)

ASSETS		
Financial Assets (Non-Retirement)		
Checking Account	$3,956	
Savings Account	15,500	
CDs	25,000	
Large Cap Mutual Fund	225,287	
Small Cap Mutual Fund	156,482	
Total Non-Retirement Financial Assets		**$426,585**
Financial Assets (Retirement)		
401(k) (Mel)	$255,728	
401(k) (Anita)	188,734	
IRA (Mel)	176,784	
IRA (Anita)	150,372	
Rollover IRA (Mel)	72,944	
Total Retirement Financial Assets		**$844,616**
Total Financial Assets		**$1,271,201**
Use Assets		
Residence	$450,000	
Furniture/Household Goods	10,000	
Vehicle #1	15.000	
Vehicle #2	12,000	
Total Use Assets		**$487,000**
TOTAL ASSETS		**1,758,201**
LIABILITIES		
Vehicle #1 Loan	4,500	
Credit Card Debt (Avg. Monthly Balance)	1,400	
Total Liabilities		**$5,900**
NET WORTH		**$1,752,301**
TOTAL LIABILITIES AND NET WORTH		**$1,758,201**

Robert and June Gordon

As a second case study, let's look at Robert and June Gordon, another fictional couple, who are at age 66 and want very much to retire. They have three children and one grandchild (so far). The mortgage loan on their house is less than $34,000 and will be paid off in seven years. They are in reasonably good health, and they expect to live well into their 80s. Take a look at their balance sheet. Their financial asset base is $559,050. Their net worth is $939,000, about one-third of which is the equity in their residence. Their liabilities are manageable.

The Gordons have decided to live comfortably in retirement and not stint on themselves in order to maximize the inheritance of their heirs. They may give some small gifts to their heirs while they are alive, but leaving a lot of money for them while not living their own lives fully in retirement is not their objective.

They would like to have an annual income of $110,000 during retirement. They expect to receive Social Security benefits of $43,127. This leaves a shortfall of $66,873 that will be made up by tapping their financial assets. But there's a problem. With financial assets of $559,050 and assuming a 6% growth rate, with an annual withdrawal of $66,873 to cover the shortfall, their financial assets will be depleted in about 11 years.

What they could do is sell their house for $375,000 and replace it with a more modest abode costing $200,000. This will add $175,000 to their financial assets, which would now total $734,050. With this starting figure, their financial assets will last 17 years. Given their anticipated longevity, the numbers just don't work.

They have some options (all computations assume a 6% yield on investments):
1. Reduce their desired retirement income to $90,000. After considering the Social Security benefits, the shortfall would now be $20,000 less, $46,873. With this starting figure, their financial assets will last 20 years.
2. Reduce their desired retirement income to $90,000, and make the house exchange as indicated above. This would increase their financial assets to $734,050. This will last for 38 years and would take them through age 104.
3. Keep working, either or both of them, part-time for additional income to help offset the shortfall.

Figure 9-2
Robert and June Gordon - Balance Sheet, March 18, 2014
(All assets and liabilities are held jointly unless otherwise specified)

ASSETS		
Financial Assets (Non-Retirement)		
Checking Account	$2,155	
Savings Account	12,400	
Savings Bonds	37,500	
Large Cap Index Mutual Fund	126,454	
International Mutual Fund	76,974	
Total Non-Retirement Financial Assets		**$255,483**
Financial Assets (Retirement)		
401(k) (Robert)	$185,311	
403(b) (June)	55,384	
IRA (Robert)	62,872	
Total Retirement Financial Assets		**$303,567**
Total Financial Assets		**$559,050**
Use Assets		
Residence	$375,000	
Furniture/Household Goods	12,000	
Vehicle #1	15.000	
Vehicle #2	18,000	
Total Use Assets		**$420,000**
TOTAL ASSETS		**979,050**
LIABILITIES		
Mortgage Loan	$33,750	
Vehicle #1 Loan	5,300	
Credit Card Debt (Avg. Monthly Balance)	1,000	
Total Liabilities		**$40,050**
NET WORTH		**$939,000**
TOTAL LIABILITIES AND NET WORTH		**$979,050**

In short, in retirement they could spend less and/or earn some income, to make up for the shortfall between their Social Security benefits and their desired expenditures. With their current financial resources, they will probably spend most of it in retirement. Their estate will comprise their house, personal property, and whatever financial assets remaining.

The Planning Process at Retirement

As shown in these two case studies, the planning process at retirement comprises four steps.
- Identify the sources of your retirement income.
- Determine the amounts available to you from these sources.
- Decide on your desired retirement income.
- Make the numbers work.

Making the numbers work means looking at all factors in order to plan an orderly drawdown of your assets to meet your goals. If the numbers don't work, you may have to change your goals. Using a financial calculator, you can determine how much money, in dollar amounts, you will need to withdraw from your asset base. This establishes a drawdown trajectory. However, any determination will depend on certain assumptions you must make, which include changes in asset values as you are drawing down the assets.

Perhaps, during retirement, your asset values increase more than expected, resulting in the dollar amounts taken represent a lower percentage of your asset base. Or perhaps, unfortunately, your asset values decrease, resulting in the dollar amounts taken represent a higher percentage of your asset base. If either of these occurrences transpires, you will have to make adjustments in the original drawdown trajectory.

How to Draw Down Your Financial Assets

As you plan to draw down your assets to finance your retirement, there are a few issues you need to address.

Liquidity

The first concern should be liquidity. As presented in Chapter Three, liquidity is defined as the ease with which an asset can be readily converted to cash. Assets that will be needed in the next few years should be liquid. Why? Because you want to avoid needing to sell an asset when that asset category (or the particular asset you want to sell) is in a slump.

You know that markets, as well as individual assets, go up and go down. You also know that, in the long run, long-term investments in equities will yield superior results than short-term fixed income investments, or cash. Thus, you want to be invested in what will give you superior results in the long run. However, for the short term, having ready cash can save you from having to sell an asset at a lower than expected price.

The most liquid assets are:
- Cash
- Savings accounts
- Money market accounts
- Short-term bonds
- Short-term certificates of deposit (CDs)

These are the financial instruments in which your needs for the next few years should be placed.

You can refine this somewhat, and increase your yield on these assets, by putting next year's needed money in cash, savings accounts, and money market accounts. At the same time, build a ladder of short-term bonds or CDs. For example, if you're going to need $15,000 in each of the next three years, buy three $15,000 lots of these instruments with maturity dates of one, two, and three years. At the end of the first year, redeem the one-year instruments when they mature. At this time, the two-year and three-year instruments become one-year and two-year instruments respectively. Then put $15,000 taken from other financial assets into instruments that mature in three years. You can keep this ladder going for years.

Tax-Deferring (or Avoiding)
Generally, when tapping your financial resources for retirement, try to delay, insofar as possible, withdrawing from tax-preferred accounts, (IRAs, 401(k)s, etc). The tax-free compounding in these accounts will allow more growth than in taxable vehicles. At age 70 ½, you will need to make Required Minimum Distributions from all of these tax-preferred investments, except for a Roth IRA.

If, when you die, there is money left in an IRA (traditional or Roth), it will pass through to the beneficiary. The taxation of inherited IRAs is very complex, depending on the relationship of the deceased to the beneficiary, as well as other factors.

What to Do with Excess Wealth

The two case studies presented above, the Coopers and the Gordons, show how to go about financing your retirement. The Gordons needed to use all their financial assets in retirement. Unless they reduce their desired income needs even more, perhaps to $70,000 annually, they will not have much left over.

On the other hand, the Coopers are in the enviable position of having more than enough money to finance their retirement. Now their dilemma is what to do with their excess wealth. Do they want to leave a large estate to their heirs? Do they want to spend it? Give it away? The problem of what to do with their excess wealth is a wonderful problem to have, but it must be thought through.

There are three things you can do with your excess financial wealth.
1. Keep it. Probably just continue with your present portfolio.
2. Spend it. This is fun, but it's not as easy as it might seem.
3. Give it away. This is really fun, but you should try to get the most bang for your buck.

You can do one, two, or all three of these things. Let's consider each of these options separately.

Keep It

If you want to keep your excess wealth, for whatever reason, you probably would do well to invest it in a diversity of assets. It may already be invested in such a way. When you shuffle off this mortal coil, your net assets will be part of your estate, and might be subject to taxation. Under current law, $5.25 million is the threshold over which the estate tax kicks in. (More about this later.) If you are averse to paying this tax, then you should seriously consider the other two options, spending your wealth and/or giving it away, in order to reduce your estate and avoid any estate tax.

Spend It

This seems easy enough. Take some money from your excess wealth and buy something for yourself with it. However, this is not always easy to do. For some folks, the wealth that they have accumulated is an integral part of their personae. Perhaps all their lives, they were frugal; they carefully invested their discretionary money, and reinvested the investments' return, never having spent much on themselves. Then, they have an epiphany: "Holy cow! I've got all this money. I know I could spend it, but should I be spending it on myself? I've never really done this before." If you have this problem, you have some soul-searching to do.

Spending Money on Yourself.

For some folks, spending money on themselves is a problem. And if you are such a person, there are three questions you must ask yourself:

1. "Can I change?" That is, do I have the ability to change? With some people, a lifetime of frugality and deferred gratification cannot be overcome. They simply cannot change these habits, and they end up exercising the two other options: keeping it, or giving away. If you can change, this leads to the second question:

2. "Do I want to change?" You might answer, "Yes, I want to change. I'd like to spend some money on myself, but I'm afraid that if I do, my life will be different in known and perhaps unknown ways, and I don't want to take a chance. I like the way my life is right now." But is this decision yours and yours alone to make? Should anyone or anything be guiding you in making this decision? This leads to the third question:

3. "Should I change?" Now, the idea of spending money on yourself takes on a moral dimension. You might ask yourself, "Is it right for me to spend money on myself for things that are not essential to my well being? I mean, there are people in the world who have nothing. They never had anything, and their future is bleak. Is it ethical for me to spend money on fluff when they have substantive needs?"

You'll have to wrestle with this issue.

When facing moral or ethical decisions, you must examine your core values. It's of interest to note that virtually all religions promote the idea of charitable giving to those in need. But in terms of giving to yourself, the moral guidelines are fewer. These are several verses in Ecclesiastes, which promote the idea of enjoying the fruits of your labor.

5:19 When God gives any man wealth and possessions, and enables him to enjoy them, to accept his lot and be happy in his work—this is a gift of God.

8:15 So, I commend the enjoyment of life, because nothing is better for a man under the sun, than to eat and drink and be glad.

Moreover, the Talmud teaches that, in the next world, your soul will have to answer for every permitted pleasure that you failed to enjoy. So, at least in the Judeo-Christian ethic, with which I am most familiar, the message is clear: Life should be enjoyed, and if you've worked hard, provided for your family, and made gifts to charity, there's nothing wrong with spending money on yourself in order to enjoy some of life's pleasures.

For those who do not have this problem, that is, those can spend money on themselves without guilt, let's explore the idea of spending on yourself.

There is Spending, and Then There is Spending.

How do you spend money on yourself? Spending money to buy something of value may lower the amount of cash you have on hand, but it isn't necessarily an expenditure. You must make a distinction between spending it, and merely changing its classification. An example should make this distinction clear.

Let's say you always wanted a second residence, perhaps in the mountains or at the beach. And now you can afford it. You and your family would really enjoy it. Here's an excerpt from your present balance sheet in a very simplified form.

ORIGINAL BALANCE SHEET

ASSETS			
	Cash	$7,000,000	
	Residence	$372,000	
Total Assets			$7,372,000
LIABILITIES			
	Assorted Debt	$6,500	
Total Liabilities			$6,5000
NET WORTH			$7,365,500

So, you decide to buy a second residence in the mountains. You find one you like for $450,000. You buy it, and (to keep this example simple) you decide to pay cash for it. You take $450,000 from your stash of cash, and plunk it down as full payment for the new house. Now, let's look at your new balance sheet:

BALANCE SHEET AFTER PURCHASE

ASSETS			
	Cash	$6,550,000	
	Primary Residence	$372,000	
	Secondary Residence	$450,000	
Total Assets			$7,372,000
LIABILITIES			
	Assorted Debt	$6,500	
Total Liabilities			$6,5000
NET WORTH			**$7,365,500**

Before the purchase of your second residence, your net worth was $7,365,500. After this purchase, your net worth is still $7,365,000. You really haven't spent anything[1], and you haven't reduced your wealth. What you've done is take $450,000 of cash, and put it in an asset worth $450,000. This is merely an exchange of assets. You haven't really spent $450,000; you've just modified the assets on your balance sheet. Your net worth is unchanged. Of course, when you move in to your new residence, you'll have to buy furniture, pay for utilities, upkeep, taxes, and so forth. That's money you'll be spending. But the purchase of the house itself is not <u>spending</u> wealth but rather, <u>reclassifying</u> it.

A true expenditure of money takes place when you shell out some dollars for something, and when it's over, all you have is the memory of the experience. How can you truly spend money? Here are some ideas:

- Take a cruise.
- Eat out more often.
- Have a massage.
- Go on an exotic vacation.
- Drink quality single malt Scotch rather than lesser brands.
- Go to the theater, the opera, the symphony, baseball games, or other things you enjoy. And get the best seats available for as many of these activities as you like, and for as many times as you like.
- Pay someone else to do jobs you don't like to do. such as mowing

---

1   Except, of course, for the fees associated with the purchase, such as closing costs, title search, etc.

the lawn, driving at night, or doing your taxes. [As an added bonus, a CPA may do a better job on your taxes than you would.]

These are ideas that will involve spending money. And implementing these ideas will decrease your asset base and lower your net worth, while adding to the enjoyment of your life.

The third activity for dispersing excess wealth is delightful: giving it away. This will be the focus of the next chapter.

Chapter Ten

Giving it Away

One of the true joys of having discretionary wealth is the satisfaction you can derive from giving it away. There is nothing quite like it. It benefits the giver as well as the receiver. Everyone wins.

Andrew Carnegie, an industrialist in the late 19th and early 20th centuries, and at that time the richest man in the world, became one of the best-known philanthropists ever. He espoused the view that anyone who died wealthy dies in disgrace. And he lived his philosophy, giving away most of his wealth before he died. For example, he funded the development of over 2,800 free public libraries. More recently, Warren Buffet and Bill Gates have each donated a good portion of their wealth to humanitarian causes. And Buffet has been influencing his fellow billionaires to pledge to do the same.

Every religion I know of makes it a basic tenet of its faith to give to those who are in need. Giving seems to be a universal commandment. But regardless of religious beliefs, to provide help those who need it, is clearly the right, moral, and ethical thing to do. So, what's the best way to proceed? You can give away your wealth to individuals or to organizations.

Gifts to Individuals

In order to make the best use of your wealth to help others, it's important to be familiar with that part of the tax code that deals with the transfer of wealth. The federal government encourages such transfers, uses its tax laws to provide incentives for donors to give, and makes it easy for donees to receive.

Taxation of estates began in 1913.[1] Gift taxes were initiated in 1932. In 1976, the estate and gift taxes were unified into one tax dealing with the transfer of wealth. Under current law, you may transfer $5.25 million of your wealth, while living or when deceased, without incurring any

---

1   Also in that year, the income tax was made permanent and the Federal Reserve Act was passed. It was a banner year for the financial folks.

tax liability.[2] You may make an annual gift of $14,000 to as many individuals as you like without any tax consequences. Other adults in your household can do likewise. Thus, for example, in a household with a husband and a wife who have four adult children, the husband can make an annual gift of $14,000 to each child, a total of $56,000 for the four of them. The wife can do the same, raising the amount given to $112,000. And they can do this in every calendar year, and not have to be concerned with taxes. Such gifting will reduce wealth quickly and efficiently. It should be noted that there are never any tax consequences for the recipients of these gifts. However, for the donors, there are some considerations.

Although there are no tax consequences to the donor for annual gifts of $14,000 or less per donor and per recipient, for gifts in excess of that amount, the excess is charged to $5,250,000 estate/gift tax exclusion. For example, if you made a gift of $100,000 in a given year to an individual, $14,000 would have no tax consequences, but the remaining $86,000 would be applied to your $5,250,000 exclusion, thus reducing the exclusion to $5,164,000. Since the $100,000 gift has potential tax consequences, in the year of the gift, you should file an IRS Form 709 to inform the IRS of the transfer.

If the gift were to be made to someone who is a potential heir, you need to decide whether the heir would be better off receiving the money now, rather than after you die. Do they need it now? By giving it away now, you will have the satisfaction of knowing that you have helped them financially at a time when they needed it. This is called "giving with a warm hand."

Educational Expenses

Section 529 of the tax code encourages saving money to be used for educational purposes. These 529 plans allow a taxpayer to put away money for a beneficiary to use for qualified educational purposes, such as tuition, fees, and books. These plans may be structured as pre-paid tuition plans, or savings plans. There is no limit on the number of beneficiaries for whom plans can be generated by one person. There is no limit on the amounts that can be placed in these accounts, except that for annual contributions over $14,000, the excess will count against

---

2   This presentation refers only to federal taxation. There are several states that levy estate and inheritance taxes at a threshold lower than that of the federal government.

the $5.25 million estate/gift tax exclusion. However, if you choose to contribute up to $70,000 in one calendar year, you may elect to treat the contribution as being given over a period of five years (five years X $14,000 = $70,000).

There is no federal tax on the earnings from these accounts. Indeed, many states allow a limited deduction from taxable income on their state income tax forms. Each state has its own plan, and there are many plans from which to choose. You need not choose the plan sponsored by your state, although if you choose another state's plan, you will not be eligible for the potential tax deduction offered by your state.

Educational and Medical Expenses
Beyond the 529 plans, you may pay for a person's educational expenses another way. You may make a payment directly to the qualified institution (not to the beneficiary), but for tuition only. Similarly, you can pay for medical expenses if the payment is made directly to the institution providing the medical services. In both cases, the payments are exclusive of the $14,000 gift limitation.

In summary then, you may make gifts directly to beneficiaries for whatever purposes they choose, you may help finance their higher education expenses through 529 plans, or you may make payments directly to educational and medical institutions for qualified expenses. By doing any or all of these things, you can make a substantial reduction to your net worth.

Gifts to Organizations
Among the many and varied components of the US Federal Tax Code is Section 501 (c) (3), which deals with gifts to qualified non-profit organizations, such as schools, churches, hospitals. These are called charitable contributions.[3] However, the manner in which you make a contribution can affect its net cost, with no negative effects to the receiving institution.

---

3 Strictly speaking, there is a difference between charity and philanthropy. Charity refers to gifts to those with immediate needs, such as food, clothing, and shelter. Philanthropy refers to gifts of a structural or more permanent nature, such as a wing of a building, a scholarship, or an endowed professorial chair. For this discussion, I'll include both terms—charity and philanthropy—within the term charity, or charitable contributions.

Donate Cash or Other Assets?

Ordinarily, a person who wants to make a charitable contribution writes out a check and gives it to the organization. However, in lieu of cash, other assets can be donated, e.g. shares of stock, a car, a house, a boat, etc. If the asset that is under consideration to be donated has appreciated while you have owned it, if you were to sell it, you might be liable for capital gains taxes on the profit. But if you give it directly to the organization, you pay no tax on the appreciation, nor does the organization. Let's see how this works.

Say you want to donate $5,000 to a qualified organization, perhaps your church or synagogue. How shall you do this? As an example, let's assume that you own stock purchased for $3,000, and that is now worth $5,000. Thus, you have a $2,000 paper profit. Let's further assume that you itemize deductions, you are in the 25% marginal tax bracket, and you are eligible for paying a 15% long-term capital gains tax. What are your options?

Option 1. Sell the stock, and give the proceeds, $5,000 in cash, to the organization. You can take the $5,000 deduction, which is worth $1,250, (25% of $5,000) against your gross income. But you'll have to pay capital gains tax on the appreciated portion of your gift, $2,000, which could be 15% or 25% depending on how long you have owned the stock.

Option 2. Give the stock worth $5,000 directly to the organization, which then sells it and gets $5,000 in cash. You take the $5,000 deduction, which is worth $1,250, but you also avoid paying the capital gains tax on the $2,000 appreciation of the stock given. This saves you money.

Long-term (LT) Holding: If you have held the stock for more than one year, the stock's appreciation ($2,000) would have been taxed at 15% or, $300 (15% of $2,000). But since you gave the stock directly to the organization, you do not have to pay the tax, nor does the organization. Thus, your $5,000 donation to the organization has a net cost to you of $3,450: donation less deduction less tax saving.

Short-term (ST) Holding: If you have held the stock for less than one year, the appreciation would have been taxed at 25%, or $500 (25% of

$2,000). But since you gave the stock directly to the organization, you do not have to pay the tax, $500. Thus, your $5,000 donation to the organization has a net cost to you of $3,250: donation less deduction less tax saving. The table below shows the comparison of donations in cash or stock.

Type of Donation	Deducation	Tax Savings	Net Cost
Cash	$1,250	none	$3,750
Stock with LT Gains	$1,250	$300	$3,450
Stock with ST Gains	$1,250	$500	$3,250

Other considerations

- Note that regardless of whether your donation is in cash or in appreciated stock, the organization will have the full $5,000 you gave. If you give appreciated stock and do not itemize deductions, you can still save by not having to pay capital gains taxes on the appreciated portion of your donation.
- If you have stock that is worth less than you paid for it, and you want to sell it, do so. Then apply the loss to any gains you may have from selling appreciated stock. It makes no sense to give this stock as a donation. Neither you nor the organization would gain from this loss.
- Donations in cash or stock held less than one year are limited to 50% of your Adjusted Gross Income (AGI). Donations in stock held more than one year are limited to 30% of your AGI. Any excess over these limitations may be carried over for a maximum of five years.
- You can give other non-cash properties to a qualified organization, such as used cars or antiques. However, there might be problems in ascertaining the fair market value of the property, and issues concerning the appropriate level of taxation.
- You may be able to specify to the receiving entity how you want your donation to be used. For example, you could make a donation to a university. In the absence of any instructions to the contrary, they will probably put it in their non-restricted general fund. That would be fine with them, if it's okay with you. However, you could specify that your donation be used for a special purpose, for example, a scholarship or a prize. You could specify the major field of study for the recipient as well

as other restrictions. You could have the scholarship named after someone, perhaps as a memorial. If you are considering a donation to any qualified organization, it would be worthwhile to ask them the details of their policies for receiving gifts. I'm sure they would be delighted to work with you on this.

Implementation

If you decide to give stock to a qualified organization, and you have the stock certificate, merely present the certificate to the receiving organization. However, most folks have their portfolios in the form of book entries in their brokerage accounts. In this case, first find out 1) the precise name of the receiving entity, 2) its account number, and 3) its DTC number.[4] Then, in writing, direct your broker to transfer the shares from your account to the receiving entity's account.

---

4   This is the Depository Trust Company number, which is used for partial account transfers between two brokers.

Chapter Eleven

Taxation: The Wild Card

You may have noticed that in this book, whenever I write about taxes, I begin with the phrase, "Under current tax law…" I do this deliberately, because tax law is constantly changing[1] and there is no end in sight. The federal government has grown immensely in the last 80 years, and continues to grow. And as the role of government expands, so must the money to finance the expansion. The money will largely be generated by taxes. This presents a problem for planners, since all decisions about your financial future must consider taxes as an important factor. What will taxes be in the future? I don't know, except that I expect that they will most likely be higher than now.

The issues of the size of government and taxation are among the nation's most divisive conflicts in the realm of politics. I do not take sides in this debate. Rather, I present the common sense notion that if the role of government expands, as it has been doing for decades, this expansion will have to be financed. The same rules of arithmetic are in effect for both Democrats and Republicans, for liberals as well as conservatives. This discussion seeks to be apolitical, but factual.

The root problem of our current taxation environment is that many Americans want the government to provide more social services and more financial assistance to them, but seem to be less inclined to tax themselves to pay for this. Our representatives in Washington, D.C., are sensitive to the desires of their constituents. So, the government continues to grow, and if there is not enough money to pay for the increased services, it borrows. As I write, the national public debt is almost $12 trillion, representing 75% of gross domestic product. And the government is seeking to increase the debt limit. (This is like increasing your credit card limits when you've maxed out your present limits. By doing so, have you solved your overspending problem?) And the federal budget has not been balanced since 1957. In the last 40 years, there have been budget surpluses in only five years.

---

1   The changes in tax code are almost always increases. In 2013 there was a rare example of a decrease when the estate tax exemption of 2001, was raised from $675,000 to $5.25 million, thus increasing the threshold over which the value of estate would be subject to taxation.

The federal tax code is more than 10,000 pages long, extremely complex, and gives a considerable amount of employment to accountants and tax lawyers, many of whom focus on tax specialties, and sub-specialties within their specialties. The idea of a comprehensive tax reform has been bandied about for as long as I can remember, and it hasn't happened yet. It may never happen.

So, the fact remains that the federal tax revenues must increase to maintain the level of governmental services desired by the people. Where will the revenue come from? The best solution for increasing revenue is to have a healthy and growing economy. This means that more citizens will be working, and thus paying payroll and income taxes. Also, an economic climate of this sort will cause a rise in the stock market. In such a situation, when business profits are rolling in, usually there are increases in the payment of dividends, which are subject to taxation. And when stocks are sold and profits taken, the revenue from capital gains taxes is increased. This is exactly what happened in the boom years of the 1990s.

However, in a slow-growth or no-growth economy, where will the needed revenue come from? It will come from the people who have it. That will probably include people who are reading this book. And how will this happen? There are two ways.
- By increasing revenue from existing taxes
- By adding new taxes.

Income Tax

The largest portion of government revenue comes from taxes people pay on their income, however derived: wages, salaries, tips, royalties, capital gains, dividends, interest (except for some interest that paid from municipal bonds), gambling winnings, and on and on. Once a tax has been levied, its rate may change, as well as the threshold of taxation. This has varied considerably in our nation's history.

Temporary income taxes were levied to finance the War of 1812, and the Civil War. In 1913, with the passage of the 16th Amendment, federal taxation of income was made permanent and, of course, continues to this day. [It is of interest to note that in 1913, the income tax rates ranged from 1% to 7%, and was levied on income in excess of $500,000. Obviously, not many people 100 years ago were subject to this tax.]

Means-Testing

The Internal Revenue Service (IRS) can easily identify taxpayers' income from their annual tax returns.[2] According to a means-testing philosophy, those taxpayers who have higher incomes (i.e., more means), and thus ostensibly can afford higher taxes, will be taxed more than those with lower incomes. This can be done in numerous ways.

Rates. The tax rate on any kind of income (earnings, dividends, interest, capital gains, rents, royalties etc.) can be raised. For example, for 2013, a couple having taxable income of more than $450,000 will have a marginal tax rate of 39.6%.[3] This could be raised to, say, 45% or even higher.

Thresholds. The point at which taxpayers are subject to tax, its threshold, can be lowered. Continuing with the previous example, the threshold of the 39.6% rate could be lowered from $450,000 to $350,000 or lower.

Deductions. Deductions (such as charitable contributions, mortgage loan interest, etc.) from gross income can be reduced or abolished. Or caps can be put on them to limit the amount deducted. The caps could come in the form of "phaseouts." For 2013, a taxpayer with a gross income of more than $300,000 will find the amount of allowable deductions beginning to be phased out, and thus becoming less valuable.

Exemptions. The personal exemptions of $3,800 could be reduced or abolished entirely. As described under deductions, for 2013, personal exemptions are subject to phaseouts as well.

Payroll taxes

Two payroll taxes now in existence are Social Security and Medicare. Both started as pure payroll taxes, that is, taxes on earned income such as wages and salaries.

Social Security

For 2013, taxpayers pay a Social Security tax of 6.2% on their wage base up to $113,700. This contribution is matched by their employers. When

---

2   Wealth, however, is more difficult to ascertain. See Chapter Two for a presentation of the difference between income and wealth.

3   In this presentation, for the sake of simplicity, all information about thresholds, exemptions, etc. is presented for married taxpayers filing jointly. Rates for single taxpayers are almost always lower, and never higher.

Social Security was begun in 1935, there was no income tax levied on its benefits. But in 1983, taxation of benefits was initiated. Under present law, for a beneficiary with gross income between $25,000 and $34,000, 50% of the benefits are subject to taxation. With income of more than $34,000, 85% of the benefits are subject to taxation.

Congress could easily do away entirely with the minimum thresholds of $25,000 and $34,000, and make the threshold zero. And they could increase the amount subject to taxation from 85% to 100%. In other words, they could tax all benefits received as if the benefits were ordinary income, such as salaries and wages.

Medicare

When initiated in 1965, a Medicare payroll tax of 1.45% (matched by the employer) was levied on earned income with no cap. Since this is not a direct cash payment to the taxpayer, but rather a payment made to providers of services, taxpayers do not pay a tax on Medicare benefits. (But of course, the recipients of Medicare payments such as doctors, hospitals, and the like, do pay taxes, so the government will get back some of their payments for Medicare through this taxation of the income of the providers.)

There is nothing to stop Congress from raising the Medicare tax. In fact, for 2013 they have done just that. For married taxpayers filing jointly with earnings $250,000 or more, the excess over $250,000 is subject to a Medicare surtax of 0.9%, which is added to the 1.45%, for a total tax of 2.35% Additionally, for these taxpayers, a Medicare tax of 3.8% will now be applied to net investment income, heretofore not included in the income base for application of the Medicare tax. So the idea of Medicare tax being purely a payroll tax is not quite as true as it was.

Eligibility for Medicare Part A (hospital costs) comes automatically with no premium at age 65. Part B (doctors' fees) must be requested separately, and is paid for by monthly premiums subtracted from Social Security benefits. The premiums for Part B are currently subject to means testing, and if the income of a Social Security beneficiary is over a certain threshold, the Part B premium is raised. This is accomplished through a reduction in the Social Security benefit.

How Shall I Tax Thee? Let Me Count the Ways.

Anything can be taxed. And if it has not yet been taxed, it may very well be in the future.

Value Added Tax (VAT)

In many countries, taxpayers pay a Value Added Tax of up to 25% on the purchase of many goods and services. This is like a national sales tax. For years, this idea has surfaced in the halls of Congress, and is presented as an alternative to our present income tax. I fear that the initiation of a VAT might morph into an addition to the income tax, rather than an alternative to it.

Intangibles Tax

Some states used to levy a tax on an individual's intangible property. This tax is an ad valorum tax on most financial assets. The way it worked is, an individual self-reported the value of his or her intangible financial assets, and a tax was levied on that amount, typically about 0.001%. Not a high rate to be sure, but it could be levied on sizable amounts of financial assets. Georgia repealed its intangibles tax in 1996, as have most other states. Perhaps the federal government might be tempted to resurrect this idea. In this way, they could tax wealth, not just income.

Municipal Bond Interest

Interest on municipal bonds (issued by states, cities, and counties) is presently exempt from federal taxation. However, for a number of years, the IRS has asked taxpayers to report how much tax-exempt interest they received. This is noted on line 8b on Form 1040. Although this amount is not used in calculating a taxpayer's tax liability, it makes one wonder, "If they want to know this information, why? And how might they use it?" It doesn't take too much creativity to imagine that somewhere, someone in the Office of Budget and Management in Washington is studying this information, and making projections as to how much revenue can be derived if this tax-exempt income were indeed taxed. [4]

---

4   In fact, tax-exempt municipal bond interest is currently being used to compute Medicare Part B premiums. This interest is added to a taxpayer's Adjusted Gross Income (AGI) to arrive at a Modified Adjusted Gross Income (MAGI). The MAGI is then used to determine the threshold over which an increase of the premium for Medicare Part B will be levied. The total Part B premium will be subtracted from the Social Security recipient's monthly payment. So, in a sense, municipal bond interest is already being taxed, albeit in a roundabout way.

Taxation of Individual Retirement Accounts (IRAs)

Under current law, the taxation of non-deductible IRAs is limited to the earnings of the contributions, which is taxed at the ordinary income rate. The original contributions to the account that were made with after-tax money are not taxable. The IRS could re-tax the original contributions if they want. Or in the case of Roth IRAs, which are funded with after-tax dollars, and whose earnings are presently exempt from taxation, they could change this arrangement and tax everything.

Conclusion

This paints a pretty dismal picture. You might think that the government would never do such things, that it would be politically impossible, let alone dirty pool, to change the rules. Of course, if it were to be done, it would not be done all at once, but rather in small increments, and possibly with present retirees grandfathered in with the existing rules. But in Washington, they can do anything they want, because they make the rules. And when the rules get in the way of what they want to do, they can change them.

By stating candidly the views expressed in this chapter, I could be accused of excess negativism or even fear mongering. But the expansion of government and its need to finance itself is a fact, not a complaint, condemnation, or criticism. Two plus two equals four whether a person likes it or doesn't.

Chapter Twelve

Seeking Financial Advice

As you try to manage your financial resources, you may find yourself in need of help. Financial planning can be complicated and perhaps confusing. Many people know what they know, but may not know what they <u>don't</u> know. And it is what they <u>don't</u> know that can undermine successful financial planning. So, they may desire the services of a financial advisor to assist them.

Finding an appropriate financial advisor requires some thought. There are several factors to be considered, and care must to be exercised in selecting someone with whom to work. There are several criteria to be considered before a decision is made:
- Trust,
- Professional Knowledge,
- Professional Experience,
- Advisor's Compensation for Services.

Trust

There must be a high level of trust between a client and his or her financial advisor. In order for advisors to render services to their clients, the clients will need to reveal much detailed personal information about their lives, families, finances, and their plans for the future. Clients must be comfortable with their advisor in revealing this sensitive information, and must have confidence that their advisor will look out for their best interests. And advisors, for their part, should make full disclosure regarding the means by which they are compensated.

Whom can you trust?

In December, 2008, the largest fraud ever perpetrated in investment circles was uncovered. The culprit was a well-known and respected figure in the field, a man who was in large part responsible for developing the technology that led to the formation of the NASDAQ. He had served as a director of the National Association of Securities Dealers (NASD) and had been on its board of governors.

He had had his own investment securities fund for almost 50 years. He was a billionaire several times over. His clients were a worldwide collection of banks, brokerage houses, hedge funds, foundations, and a veritable Who's Who of individual investors. And he lost a lot of his clients' money as he conducted his business as a huge Ponzi scheme.

I am, of course, referring to Bernie Madoff.

One would think that a man of his experience and wealth, with a roster of ostensibly sophisticated clients, would be someone who could be trusted. I mean, if you can't trust someone with Madoff credentials, whom can you trust?

But as it turns out, he wasn't worthy of trust. He was a sophisticated thief, and is now serving time in prison with a release date in the next century. Some people just have larceny in their hearts and are able to fool a lot of clients into trusting them.

There are three lessons to be learned from the Madoff scandal.

First, if it doesn't make sense, there's something wrong. The returns received by Madoff's clients were consistently positive, year after year. This never happens in real life. The SEC was warned ten years before his apprehension that Madoff's returns were just not possible. The feckless SEC ignored the warning. The immutable law, the positive correlation of risk and reward, has not been repealed, nor will it ever be. If positive investment results occur year after year, there must be some extensive risk there at least sometimes. And if there is risk, sometimes you lose. And if you never lose, something's wrong. Definitely not kosher.

Second, when you turn your money over to someone and don't ask questions as to why the results, positive or negative, occurred, you are exercising your faith, not your logic.

And third, if you plan to hand over much of your assets to an investment professional to manage, it would be prudent to divide the assets between two or more individuals. This is the old diversity idea.

Professional Knowledge

Financial advisors often come to their profession from a variety of

backgrounds such as
- Accounting,
- Investing,
- Insurance,
- Law.

Each of these areas of endeavor has something to do with financial advising, but no one of them represents the totality of a client's needs. Financial advisors must be educated in selected aspects of all these fields in order to serve their clients effectively. Successful completion of a college level program in financial planning can give clients reasonable assurance that a given advisor has requisite knowledge to provide services for clients. However, merely being licensed to practice law, or have a Certified Public Accountant designation, or an insurance license, or investment credentials will not necessarily provide that assurance.

In financial advising, as is the case in other endeavors, the pursuit of monetary compensation is a key factor in determining the activities of an advisor. This is understandable. Advisors have to make a living just as the rest of us do. But what do they base their advice on? Often, their advice is based on what they know, and how they make a living. This is just common sense.

When a person with a medical problem asks a surgeon for advice on a medical issue, the surgeon might be inclined to recommend a surgical solution. If a chiropractor were consulted for the same problem, he might be inclined to align the spine by manipulation of the vertebrae. A faith healer might be expected to recommend prayer and the laying on of hands. People tend to view solutions for problems in the context of their training and experience.

So it is with financial advisors. If you have a financial problem, and you take it to an insurance agent, he will probably recommend a solution that employs insurance products. A lawyer might seek legal solutions. A stockbroker might recommend some financial instruments, which oddly enough, are the very instruments he sells. No surprises here.

Professional Experience

As compared to other areas of financial services, financial advising as a distinct profession is relatively new. It has attracted capable persons, many of whom are fairly young and, as a result, lack experience. A financial advisor who has experienced down markets as well as up markets, who has seen the historical development of financial planning over a period of years, and who has had personal experience with the many aspects of financial planning, is in a better position to serve clients than a planner who has not.

Compensation for Services

Advisors are compensated for their services in different ways. Some sell financial products and are compensated through commissions received from the sale of such products. Others are compensated on a fee basis. Clients must choose advisors on the basis of what form of advisor compensation is most appealing to them.

The issue of an advisor's compensation may be the most critical factor of all. First, let's be blunt: Nobody works for nothing (unless this is pro bono work). The key question a potential client must ask a potential financial advisor is:

- Who pays you? or
- How are you compensated for your services?

These questions may be summarized by asking:

- For whom do you work?

The person or organization that signs the check for the advisor's work is the entity for which the advisor works. If you sign the check, that advisor is working for you. If not, there may be a conflict of interest, as the advisor might very well have the interests of her employer or herself first, and your interests second.

Types of Financial Advisors

Stock Brokers/Portfolio Managers

Virtually all full-service financial brokerage firms (e.g. USB, Citigroup) have research departments. Ostensibly, the role of the analysts is to research the financial instruments in their purview, and to make buy and sell recommendations to institutions, as well as retail clients, like you and me. No problem so far.

But brokerage firms engage in a variety of other services. They can act as market-makers for some type of securities. They can engage in other investment banking activities, such as underwriting public offerings of stock, for which they receive hefty fees. Here's where there can be some problems.

There is supposed to be a "Chinese wall" between the firm's research department and its other activities. This is supposed to maintain the objectivity of the research analysts by not allowing other business interests of the firm to influence analysts' research findings and recommendations. Great idea. But this wall is sometimes breached, and the integrity of the analysts is then compromised.

Enron

A particularly egregious example of this type of breach was chronicled by Kurt Eichenwald, a *New York Times* journalist. His book, *Conspiracy of Fools*, tells the story of the fall of Enron. The story would be unbelievable, if it weren't true. Here's the short version of Enron's activities that are germane to this discussion.

In the 1990s, Andy Fastow was the Chief Financial Officer of Enron, whose stock was often used by Enron in a variety of financial transactions as collateral for loans. As long as the stock price was stable or higher, Enron was secure in its participation in these events. John Olson, an analyst with Merrill Lynch, one of the largest and most well known of Wall Street's firms, had written several reports on Enron that were "neutral or vaguely positive." Indeed, Olson cut his rating of Enron's stock.

Fastow called Merrill and told them that they were not going to be co-managers of a stock offering Enron was planning. Now, participating in a stock offering as a manager is a very lucrative activity. The fees that Merrill would have received would be enormous. Merrill asked why they were being shut out from the offering. Fastow said that it was because of John Olson and his less-than-glowing research reports on Enron. A month later, Olson was fired from Merrill. Not Merrill's finest hour.

A few months later, Enron was to have an initial public offering of a recent acquisition, Azurix, a water company. Merrill was to be the lead underwriter, no doubt a reward for dumping Olson. Solomon Smith Barney (SSB) was another Wall Street behemoth. One of their analysts,

Don Dufresne, had been somewhat tentative in his reporting on Enron, which he said had potential, but also some risk. Fastow got on the phone to SSB and complained that Dufresne had been too cautious in his ratings of Enron. So, SSB was given a trivial role in the offering. A few months later, Dufrense was gone from SSB and another, more compliant, analyst was assigned to cover Enron. Like Merrill, this was not SSB's finest hour.

So, on Wall Street the word was out: If you are an analyst and are negative about Enron, you might lose your job. So much for the Chinese wall.

Both Merrill and SSB wanted to do investment banking for Enron. They knew on which side of their bread was buttered. They sacrificed their integrity for the sake of profits. Misinformation or incomplete information was given to their retail customers. They were the losers.

Had shenanigans like this ever occurred before the Enron debacle? Certainly. Are they going on now? No doubt. Will they go on in the future? Probably. Times change, names change, but human nature does not.

The point of this extended discussion of Enron throwing its weight around the investment banking industry is that a financial advisor associated with an investment bank may or may not giving you worthwhile advice. Advisors and the firms they represent should make a full disclosure of their relationship with a stock they are recommending. Do they own it? Many Wall Street firms, as well as advisors who are independent of them, are beginning to make such disclosures as a matter of course.

Financial Planners

There is a group of financial advisors who are financial planners. They have been educated in all aspects of personal finance: investments, insurance, taxation, and estate planning. Some are certified, having passed a rigorous written test and having had experience in the financial field. They have the Certified Financial Planner (CFP) designation.

All financial planners are compensated for their services in one of three different ways.

No-fee Planners: Some planners are insurance agents who sell insurance products to clients and are compensated by the commissions they receive. There are also stockbrokers or mutual fund salespersons who are compensated similarly. These persons generally work for insurance agencies, brokerage houses, banks, mutual fund companies, and similar businesses. They charge no fees to their clients because they receive commissions on the products they sell, or salaries from their employers. That is their compensation.

Fee-based planners: Some planners who sell financial products to their clients develop a financial plan for them for a specified fee. Then, they sell financial products to these clients, and the commissions received from these sales offset the specified fee, sometimes reducing it substantially. They distinguish themselves from No-Fee Planners by the specified fee they charge for the plan, although the actual fee paid by clients may be much less than the original fee. Thus, their compensation is a mixture of commissions and client fees.

Fee-only Planners: Some planners charge a fee for their services, an hourly rate and/or a flat fee, and do not sell any financial products. Such planners work for, and are accountable only to their clients, and they receive their fees for services directly from them. They do not sell any financial products. They receive no commissions, no kickbacks, and no referral fees. They are independent of any brokerage house, bank, insurance company, legal or accounting firm. Thus, they serve purely in an advisory capacity. When the purchase of financial products is recommended to meet client needs, they recommend the most effective and cost-efficient provider of those products.

Some financial planners manage their clients' assets as well as provide planning services. They are usually compensated by a percentage of the assets under their management, as well as their fees.

Why is the Method of Compensation Important?

The answer is simple and can be expressed succinctly: **potential conflict of interest**. Simply put, for planners to give financial advice, and then to have their compensation based upon commissions received from the sale of the very financial products they recommend, is an invitation to mischief. Economics is, in many ways, the study of incentives. And when judgment is influenced by financial incentives, there could exist a condition known as moral hazard.

However, bear in mind that many financial planners who are no-fee and fee-based are decent people of integrity who have their clients' interests at heart. They have a wealth of information and experience to share with their clients, and are happy to do so. But they must be compensated as we all must. The conflict of interest arises when the compensation to be received from the sale of a financial product influences the advice that is given. And that could happen very easily. It's caused by human nature.

As examples:
- An advisor/insurance agent will be inclined to recommend products such as annuities and whole life policies on which she makes fat commissions, when all the client really needs is term insurance, for which she is compensated very modestly.
- An advisor/mutual funds representative will be inclined to recommend to the client mutual funds on which he receives a commission, load funds, rather than no-load funds that pay no commission to him. This is notwithstanding the fact that generally, no-load funds perform as well or better than load funds.

Concluding Thoughts

When an advisor's livelihood depends on the commissions received by clients, it is natural to expect that the advice given to clients will include the purchase financial products that yield commissions. That's why full disclosure on the part of the financial planner regarding compensation is essential.

Whether a no-fee, fee-based, or a fee-only financial planner will give sound, unbiased advice to a client is a function of the planner's knowledge and integrity. Of course, honesty, integrity, character, and other human attributes will vary from planner to planner, regardless of their compensation model. Just bear in mind that the love of money can be the root of an awful lot of evil.

Appendices

Appendix A

Cash Flow and Budgeting
(Excerpted from the author's
The Young Adult's Guide to Financial Success)

The analysis of your income and expenses will result in a Cash Flow Statement. The format for this statement is a simple one:
- List income by source. How much cash is coming in and from where?
- List expenses by function. How much cash is going out, to whom, or for what?
- Subtract the expenses from the income, and the result is your cash flow.

This statement should be done for a year, usually the last full calendar year. In other words, last year how much money came in, where did it go? To develop your first Cash Flow Statement will require some time and effort. But in subsequent years, the format will already have been set up, and modifications will involve merely making adjustments to the previous year's statement.

What's In This Statement?
Here are some of the items needed for a Cash Flow Statement. You'll notice that virtually all of the possible sources of income and types of expenditures are listed. I don't expect that you'll use even half of them. But they are listed so you don't forget anything. Try to be as complete as you can.

Income
This should be fairly easy to do. List the sources and amounts. The salary amount should be the gross amount, your actual salary, not your take home pay. This can be readily ascertained by examining your pay statement. Don't include any one time/non-recurring monies received, such as an inheritance or a gift.

Income items: salaries, fees, tips, self-employment income, dividends, capital gains, trust income, alimony received, child support received, other income (specify).

Expenses

This is a much longer list, since you will probably have many more expenses than sources of income. I don't expect you to use all of these items. Select those that are applicable to your household. Provide the information with as much accuracy as possible.

To save some time in estimating recurring items whose payments may differ from month to month such as utilities, select three typical months such as February, June and October, total the payments made in those months and multiply by four. Then enter that amount in your analysis. Sometimes estimates will have to be made. That's fine. Just be as accurate as you can.

Expense Items

alimony paid	cable/satellite TV	car fuel
car insurance	car loan payments	car repairs/maintenance savings
cell phone	child support	clothing
credit card interest	dining out	education
electricity	entertainment	federal income taxes
FICA/Medicare	food	gas
gifts (charitable)	gifts (non-charitable)	health insurance
house insurance	house maintenance	rent
medical/dental expenses	mortgage loan payment (principal and interest)	new investments
professional expenses (accounting, legal, etc)	personal care	property tax
retirement plans	state income taxes	student loan payments
telephone	water/sewage	vacations
veterinary expenses	other expenses (specify)	

Don't Double Count

Be careful when you categorize expenses that you don't duplicate or overlap. For example, you might use your credit card to purchase clothing items or vacation-specific expenses such as airline tickets. Those expenses should be categorized as clothing or vacations, respectively. The only credit card expense occurs only when you don't pay off the monthly balance, and you have to pay interest.

Itemize each source of income and each category of expense. Add up your income, subtract your expenses, and the result should be your net cash flow, that is your discretionary cash.

Beware of Excessive Expenses from Pocket Money
If you find yourself in the position of going through large amounts of pocket money and not knowing where it is going, try this: For one month, a typical month of the year, track your cash expenditures. For every outgo of cash over $1, make a note of the amount and the purpose. You'd be surprised at what you might find out at the end of the month. One client of mine realized that she was spending $4 every workday morning on a cup of gourmet coffee. Do the math: $4 times 5 workdays in the week is $20 dollars per week. In 50 weeks of work this amounted to $1,000 for the year. She hadn't even realized how much she was spending that much on coffee.[1]

Cigarette smokers spend copious amount of money on their habit. A pack of cigarettes costs about $4. Again, do the math. A two pack a day smoker will spend $8 per day, or $1,460 per year. Add to that the increase in health problems associated with smoking, and the reduced life expectancy of smokers, this nicotine habit is expensive indeed.

When you've done an analysis of your cash flow, the bottom line—income minus expenses—will reveal whether your cash position is positive or negative. If it is positive, congratulate yourself. You're living within your means, and perhaps you can make it even more positive. If it is negative, then you have some work to do.

Budgeting
A budget is a plan for spending. Every business has a budget for its coming year. They anticipate their revenues and expenses, and make sure that there is positive cash flow for the year. You, too, need to do this.

To develop a budget, start with your cash flow statement. Last year's income and expenditures income are shown there.

Total Pay or Take-Home Pay?
If you want to simplify things, and if your income is derived from wages

---

1   A coffee addicted journalist figured out that a barrel of Starbuck's latte costs about $1,200. Oil, at $140 a barrel, seems rather inexpensive by comparison.

or salaries from which deductions are made (income tax withholding, FICA, pension contributions, etc), use your net income, that is, your take-home pay as the income portion of your budget. But then, of course, be sure not to include the payroll deductions in the expense portion of the budget. If you do this in the simplified form, be sure that you are aware of your employment sponsored retirement contributions. They are an important part of your net worth and your future. They will reduce your take-home pay, but you need to keep your eye on this to ensure that you are taking full advantage of these retirement benefits, and that they are growing appropriately. I prefer the non-simplified way because it shows more clearly what's going on, and it is that version which is presented below.

Now let's focus on your expenses (this includes your analysis of your small cash expenditures such as for gourmet coffee).

How Much Is Enough, and How Much Is Too Much?
Look at your Cash Flow Statement. Are there any places where you are spending money unwisely? Is your rent more than 30% of your gross income? Maybe you need a less expensive apartment. Do you need both a cell phone and a landline? Could one or the other meet you needs? Can any other expenses be reduced? Are there other expenses that you'd like to increase? Are there any expenses that might increase through no fault of yours such as increases in electricity or food costs? If so, add 5% or so to the figure from last year's cash flow statement. This is called *positive padding*, and it gives you a margin of error.

Construct Your Budget
Now, extend last year's Cash Flow Statement to this year's budget, making modifications as needed. Then, add up your budgeted expenses. They should be less than the income received, thus yielding a positive cash flow. If they are not, that is, if your cash flow will be negative, you'll need to either increase your income, or reduce your expenses, or both.

If your budget is to be a helpful plan, it should be realistic and flexible. Modify your budget accordingly, making adjustments as needed before you begin the year. What you are aiming for is to start the year with balanced budget, in which you know how much money is coming in, and what you plan to do with it. Be prepared to make further modifications as the year progresses.

Appendix B

Required Minimum Distribution (RMD) From IRAs and 401(k)s

This table, based on the IRS's longevity estimates, is used to determine the amount of Required Minimum Distributions from an IRA or a 401(k). It is meant for an individual account owner. If the account owner is married, and the spouse is more than ten years younger than the owner and is the sole beneficiary of the account, a separate table is provided by the IRS.

To determine your RMD for a given year, add together the previous year's December 31 balances of all traditional (non-Roth) IRAs for each individual. Use this figure to determine the RMD for that individual. For 401(k)s, the RMD from each account must be computed separately.

To use the table, locate the age of the owner, and divide the account balance by the divisor shown under Distribution Period. The result will be the RMD. For example, if the December 31 account balances of the owner's IRAs is $196,425, and the owner is 70 years old, divide $196,425 by 27.4. The figure, $7,169, is the RMD for that year.

RMD Calculation Table

Age	Distribution Period	Age	Distribution Period
70	27.4	93	9.6
71	26.5	94	9.1
72	25.6	95	8.6
73	24.7	96	8.1
74	23.8	97	7.6
75	22.9	98	7.1
76	22.0	99	6.7
77	21.2	100	6.3
78	20.3	101	5.9
79	19.5	102	5.5
80	18.7	103	5.2
81	17.9	104	4.9
82	17.1	105	4.5
83	16.3	106	4.2
84	15.5	107	3.9
85	14.8	108	3.7
86	14.1	109	3.4
87	13.4	110	3.1
88	12.7	111	2.9
89	12.0	112	2.6
90	11.4	113	2.4
91	10.8	114	2.1
92	10.2	115 and over	1.9

Appendix C

Fraud, Deceit, and Other Mischief

There exists a stratum of society that makes its living engaging in fraud and deceit. There is an infinity of ways in which people can be bilked. I am constantly amazed at the ingenuity of people who live their lives in a moral vacuum, and prey upon others to get their money. Rather than apply their intelligence and creativity to legal and ethical ways of making money, they choose a different route to wealth: they engage in shoddy and sometimes illegal activities.

In Chapter Twelve, I related the stories of Enron's inappropriate pressuring of investment banks, and Bernie Madoff's massive fraud. This appendix will present some of the ways in which this underworld of financial characters operates. Let's start with the well-known Ponzi Scheme.

Ponzi Schemes

Carlo Pietro Giovanni Guglielmo Tebaldo Ponzi, aka Carles Ponzi, emigrated from Italy to the United States in 1903. A few years later, he was employed by a bank in Montreal, which paid 6% on deposits while other banks at the time were paying about 3%. However, Ponzi's bank had made some bad loans and was in financial difficulty. To solve their problems, yet maintain the above-average interest paid on deposits, they started paying the 6% interest on its older, established accounts by using funds deposited in newly opened accounts. Shortly thereafter, the bank failed and most depositors lost their money. After leaving the bank, Ponzi was later arrested for forgery, served jail time, and then later got involved with an illegal immigration scheme for which he again served jail time. No honest man, he.

Later, he found his way to Boston, and using the techniques employed by the Montreal bank, he developed a scheme whereby he would promise investors he would double their investment in 90 days. He told them he would buy "postal reply coupons" at one price and sell them a higher price—an arbitrage procedure. Investors put up their money and received their promised returns. The way he did this was to pay off the original investors with the initial investments from subsequent investors, and on and on with other generations of investors. And that is the classic fraud that bears his name: the Ponzi Scheme.

Obviously, sooner or later, the scammer runs out of suckers, er, investors, and the scam is exposed for what it is.

The take-away from this brief presentation of a Ponzi scheme is summarized in three aphorisms:
- If an investment seems to good to be true, it probably is.
- The axiom stating the high correlation of risk and reward is still valid.
- When the tide goes out, you find out who's been swimming naked.[1]

Affinity Scams

A special twist on scams are those done by people you know, or with whom you have something in common. These are called affinity scams. Some of the most flagrant violations of trust are often done by people you think you know and can trust. It could be someone endorsed by your minister, priest, rabbi, or imam. Or it could be done by the clergyperson himself or herself. In this kind of operation, typically a member of your affinity group (religious organization, ethnic group, or neighborhood group, etc.), whom you have no reason to distrust, takes advantage of you by engaging in a series of fraudulent transactions. Bernie Madoff used his affinity with certain groups of people to engage in his Ponzi scheme.

Window Dressing

Mutual fund managers generally send quarterly reports to their shareholders that show their portfolio holdings as of the date of the report, the record date. These managers want to show their present shareholders and potential future shareholders what a good job they have done.[2] So, prior to the record date, they might rid the portfolio of its losers and laggards, and add high flyers to it. For example, during the quarter the fund might have held the stock of ABC Company, the price of which declined 40%. So, before the record date, they sell ABC and replace it with a purchase of XYZ stock, which has gained 65% during the quarter. This improves the appearance of the portfolio, and shows the supposed wisdom of the decisions made by the managers. This kind of portfolio enhancement is known as window dressing.

---

1 Attributed to Warren Buffet
2 Of course, the better indication of the managers' talent would be shown in the improvement of the fund's share price and the dividends paid, compared to a benchmark, say, the S&P 500 index.

There would probably be no mention of the eleventh hour transactions in ABC or XYZ in the narrative, or the footnotes accompanying the portfolio presentation. So, the casual observer of the portfolio might well have the impression that XYZ stock had been in the portfolio for the entire quarter. Is this a crime? Is this a fraud? No, it's just a misleading activity engaged in by managers who don't define the truth as including the whole truth. It is first class subterfuge, but there's no law against it.

There are, of course, variations of window dressing. One is risk shifting, whereby managers adjust their portfolios to reduce their holdings in high-risk securities to make their portfolios appear more conservative than they really have been. Another is portfolio pumping, whereby managers increase the value of their existing holdings by buying more shares of them. They are pumping up the prices of these shares, thus increasing their value.

So window-dressing by portfolio managers carries on. But, it doesn't have to be this way. It is of interest to note that Value Line, a weekly investing newsletter, presents four model portfolios, each with a different investment objective. A given stock's inclusion in a portfolio is based upon Value Line's analysis and rating system. In some weeks there are changes made, and in some weeks there are no changes. When a change is made in a portfolio by removing a stock from it, the reason for its removal is given, and the reason for its replacement is also given. There is nothing opaque there. It's all open, above board, and fully disclosed.

Insider Trading
Most professional investors, hedge fund managers and other financial folks do their research and analysis, and then make appropriate investment decisions. Some of them, however, seek an edge such as inside (non-public) information to allow them to profit at the expense of other investors.

In 2009, Raj Rajaratnam (RR), manager of Galleon Fund, a large hedge fund, was arrested on multiple counts of conspiracy and securities fraud. He had had three sources of inside information, including one who was on the board of directors of Goldman Sachs (GS), the largest investment bank on Wall Street. According to the story, the GS mole would call RR right after a GS directors meeting, and tip off RR with inside information. This allowed RR to buy or sell securities to his profit before the GS board meeting information had been disseminated.

In 2013, RR pled not guilty, but was convicted of fourteen counts of conspiracy and securities fraud. He was sentenced to eleven years in prison. He is not a healthy man and will probably die in prison before his sentence is complete.

So, between some of the brokerage houses, investment banks, and hedge funds, there are a lot of bad things happening on Wall Street.

Newsletter scams

With the cost of bulk mail as low as it is, scammers can use investment newsletters to perpetrate a variety of wicked plots against gullible investors. My favorite is the ingenious use of positive results from stock recommendations to entice paid subscriptions from newsletter recipients. There are many variations on this theme. Here's the way one might work.

The scammer starts with a long list of investors who are potential subscribers, say, 100,000 of them. She develops a biweekly newsletter and sends it to all investors on the list. She touts the newsletter as a way to achieve great wealth by following her stock picks, and offers investors a free four-issue trial subscription. Each issue, she promises, will have a great stock tip.

But first, she divides the investor list into ten groups of 10,000 each. Each group will get the newsletter, but each with a different stock recommendation. So, in the original mailing to ten different groups, there are ten different stocks recommended. Of these ten stocks, let's say four have had an increase in their value since the publication of the newsletter. So, she sends out the next mailing to only those four groups that had winning stocks. In this mailing, another ten stocks were recommended. And of these ten stocks there are, let's say three are winners.

Then she takes the groups that now have had two winning stocks, and continues this procedure for a couple more iterations until she has a group of investors who have received four stock tips, all of which resulted in positive gains. We'll call them the Final Group. Then she lowers the boom.

She sends a letter to each investor in the Final Group stating that she hopes that they followed through with her recommendations and gained financially from them. Then she goes on to write something like, "Look, I've sent you four winning recommendations. I've proved to you that I'm an excellent stock picker. You could have made a lot of money by following my recommendations. Now, you've had four free issues. But this newsletter needs revenue to survive. And so I'm asking that you subscribe to the newsletter in order to continue receiving it. For a fee of only $759, you'll receive a full year's subscription, and continue to receive my stock picks."

Now this is a sophisticated scam. It makes Ponzi look like a mere amateur.

Internet/Telephone Scams

Scams by strangers have been happening since the beginning of time. Unsolicited phone calls from scammers are omnipresent. With the addition of the Internet to the scammers' tools, their repertoire of unsavory activities is increased. And then, throw in possibility of payment by electronic means, and the stage is set for a multitude of bad players to ply their pernicious trade.

Often, these scams are focused on senior citizens, but anyone is susceptible to them. Here are a few examples.

- Free Lunch Investment Seminars. Go have lunch, on them, and then be subjected to a high-pressure sales pitch to purchase financial instruments, whether or not they appropriate for you.
- Medicare Fraud. Receive a call from someone purporting to be a government employee, asking for personal and medical information. Then they bill Medicare for services that were never rendered. Medicare fraud is widespread and is a billion dollar industry.
- Sweepstakes Winner. You are contacted by someone who tells you that you've won a sweepstakes competition. All you need to do is send in some money to claim it. Yeah, right.
- Grandparent Scam. You have a grandchild who is traveling abroad, and you receive a call from someone who says he is your grandchild and who relates a sad story of how he was robbed of all his money. Would you please send him some?

- <u>Sob Stories</u>. You get an email from an unknown source relating a touching story of how this person has been swindled out of money and needs some cash to sue the alleged swindler.

This is only a sample of possible scams from total strangers. How do you protect yourself from these? First, remember that there is no such thing as a free lunch from a stranger. Second, anyone you don't know who wants you to give him money should arouse your suspicion. And third, if you ever do send money to anyone for anything, use a credit card, and not a debit card. If you use a debit card, the cash in your account is immediately encumbered. With a credit card, a fraudulent payment may be contested, and the credit card issuer may assist you in getting your money back. In other words, with a credit card you have recourse, but with a debit card you may be just out of luck.

Index